ARCHITECTURAL
ORNAMENTALISM

ARCHITECTURAL
ORNAMENTALISM
DETAILING IN THE CRAFT TRADITION

Jim Kemp
Photographs by **Robert Perron**

WHITNEY LIBRARY OF DESIGN
An imprint of Watson-Guptill Publications
New York

A RUNNING HEADS BOOK

Library of Congress Cataloging-in-Publication Data

Kemp, Jim.
    Architectural ornamentalism.

    Includes index.
    1. Architecture—United States—Details.
2. Decoration and ornament, Architectural—United
States. I. Perron, Robert. II. Title.
NA2840.K46   1987   728'.0973   87-10670
ISBN 0-8230-7039-5

ARCHITECTURAL ORNAMENTALISM: Detailing in the Craft Tradition
was prepared and produced by
Running Heads Incorporated,
42 East 23rd Street,
New York, N.Y. 10010

Editor: Jill Herbers
Designer: Sue Rose

Typeset by David E. Seham Associates
Color separations by Hong Kong Scanner Craft Company Ltd.
Printed and bound in Hong Kong by Leefung-Asco Printers Ltd.

First published in the United States
by Whitney Library of Design,
an imprint of Watson-Guptill Publications,
a division of Billboard Publications, Inc.,
1515 Broadway, New York, N.Y. 10036

First Printing, 1987
1 2 3 4 5 6 7 8 9/92 91 90 89 88 87

To Susan Mellon and Richard Horn

ACKNOWLEDGMENTS

In our exploration of architectural crafts, we have been aided by a number of people who offered us the benefit of their expert guidance. For their enthusiastic help and entree into this exciting world we offer our sincerest thanks. We are indebted to Susan Mellon, who steered us toward the architectural crafts through her work with the Creative Arts Workshop in New Haven, Connecticut, and who personally piloted Bob Perron to many of the installations in her airplane. We also owe a deep gratitude to Joy Wulke, much of whose work is part of the fabric of Bob's own house.

We also thank the owners and representatives of craft-oriented galleries for introducing us to many of the craftspeople whose work is illustrated in this book. They include the Snyderman Gallery in Philadelphia, where the work of Dale Broholm and Joe Beyer can be viewed; the Helen Drutt Gallery, also of Philadelphia, for showing us the ceramic designs of Paula Winokur; Warren and Bernice Rubin, owners of the Workbench in New York City for guiding us to Ed Zucca; Ten Arrow Gallery in Cambridge, Massachusetts, where me met Joel Schwartz; and Judith Schulze of Modern Masters in New York City for leading us to Sherry Schreiber. In addition, we thank art consultant Susan Daniel of New Haven, through whom we met Sandra Farrell and Tim Prentice.

We also wish to thank the resource centers across the country that promote and exhibit the exciting work of today's craftspeople. In particular, we would like to note the help of the Creative Arts Workshop of New Haven, for introducing us to Ken von Roenn and Al Garber; Elena Canavier, director of the Public Art Trust in Washington, D.C., who is responsible for showing us the work of Howard Ben Tré; the National Ornamental Metal Museum in Memphis, Tennessee, where we became familiar with Dimitri Gerakaris; the Southeastern Center for Contemporary Art (SECCA) in Winston-Salem, North Carolina, where the work of Bob Trotman, Ron Propst, and Ira Dekoven has been exhibited; and Claire Holliday of the Southwest Craft Center in San Antonio, Texas, for her help in showing the crafts of Isaac Maxwell, Dorothy Davis, Bruce Duderstadt, Bill McDonald, and Ceramic Design.

For their help in leading us to Davis Wilson and Denise Leone, we thank the architectural firm of Quinn Associates in New Britain, Connecticut. And for contributing a number of projects in both the wood and glass chapters, we offer a sincere thank you to architect Bill Lipsey of Aspen, Colorado.

Our journey through the world of architectural crafts has been assisted by others who graciously gave of their time and expertise. We extend our sincerest appreciation to Laura Cehanowicz Tringali of the American Artisan Press in Brewster, New York, for seeing in our raw materials the possibility for a book on contemporary architectural detailing. Thanks, too, are in order for Carl Lehmann-Haupt, who conceived the original graphic design, and Edwin Kunz for executing Carl's vision into layouts that could be presented to potential publishers.

We'd also like to thank Linda Dell, who helped with compiling source information, and much more.

There would be no book if it had not been for the enthusiastic support and sympathetic understanding of our project by the staff of Running Heads Incorporated, of New York City under whose auspices *Architectural Ornamentalism* was written. Our heartfelt appreciation is extended to Marta Hallett, who renewed our spirits with four simple words: ''I can sell this.'' We would also like to thank other professionals at Running Heads for believing in our efforts, including Ellen Milionis, for her budgetary *ledgerdemain* that saw a book with only some color become one in full color; Mary Forsell, who, with grace and charm, gave guidance with much of the early work; that jewel among editors, Jill Harper Herbers; and our patient and long-suffering art director, Sue Rose.

Finally, we are deeply indebted to Julia Moore and Glorya Hale, our editors at Whitney Library of Design in New York City, for believing in our undertaking and facilitating its preparation.

CONTENTS

INTRODUCTION

Architectural detailing is an increasingly assertive and integral design element. Gone are the days when modern architectural styles dictated that interiors be white and that structures be devoid of ornament. Indeed, new houses are being designed specifically to include a rich array of ornamental effects, from exquisitely carved woodwork to exciting stone fireplaces and eye-catching window treatments.

Many older, architecturally mundane houses hastily erected during the late 1940s and 1950s are undergoing extensive remodeling to meet the needs of new owners. In the process, they are being distinguished from their neighbors by the addition of details that range from floor treatments to leaded-glass windows.

The revival of detailing is not limited to interiors. Exterior detailing in the form of cupolas, columns, latticework, porches, and fences is prevalent in many new and remodeled houses. And a resurgence of interest in gardening, outdoor living, and entertaining has prompted many homeowners to enliven their yards and gardens with gazebos, decks, and gates.

Of course, the practice of embellishing architecture with decorative flourishes is not new. The tradition stretches back to the earliest civilizations. Detailing was also very much a part of the ancient classical world. The Greeks and Romans both produced details that are emulated today, such as a range of columns and friezes. In fact, detailing has been such a pervasive part of architecture and ornamentation that not even the Dark Ages could kill it. As Robert Jensen and Patricia Conway point out in their book, *Ornamentalism* (Clarkson N. Potter, 1982), leaded-glass windows of the cathedrals of medieval Europe were not only appreciated for their beauty but served an educational purpose by illustrating, and thus teaching, the Gospel to illiterate worshipers.

Detailing has been deeply ingrained in architecture and design in America. Greek Revival, regarded as the first national architectural style in the United States, was based on classical motifs that used many decorative effects borrowed and adapted from the ancient world. The Industrial Revolution of the nineteenth century, especially in America and Great Britain, spurred the embellishment of houses and furniture with an abundance of details. With handy pattern books available for design inspiration and machines to do the laborious job of cutting, carpenters and cabinetmakers could incorporate any number of decorative flourishes into their work. The ease of adding details resulted in over-decoration and shoddy workmanship during the Middle Victorian Age.

Not unexpectedly, this led to a revolt in both architecture and design. The first manifestation of this reaction was the English Arts and Crafts Movement, whose adherents rejected mass production in favor of the delicacy that results from handcraftsmanship.

The emergence of modern architecture in the early twentieth century represented something else. It was an attempt to gain control over the machine by coming to terms with it. Modern architects embraced mechanization for its ability to produce massive quantities of building materials rapidly and uniformly. In some circles, the machine became a model for modern living. The house itself was envisioned by Le Corbusier as a "machine for living," with no room for superfluous decorating and nonfunctional elements. Streamlined white walls and durable materials adapted from industry were favored; delicate natural materials and flourishes not industrially inspired were spurned. The strictures against detailing and decoration were so great that the Viennese architect Adolph Loos proclaimed, "Ornament is crime."

Even during these years, however, detailing did not die completely and was often incorporated into modern architecture. For example, houses by Frank Lloyd Wright are rich in custom woodwork and furnishings.

Today, architectural detailing is being enjoyed in and of itself. Architects and owners are using visually enticing elements to enliven bland boxes inherited from the past or to imprint new houses with the owners' personalities.

Detailing is taking many and varied forms. A popular trend for the past decade has been to buy authentic antique details rescued from buildings that were otherwise destined for demolition. This way, they are given a second life that allows them to bring delight to the eyes of yet another generation.

Details are recycled and sold to the public by commercial ventures known generally as "architectural salvage yards," which have in recent years proliferated across the country. Regardless of the extent of one's interest in detailing, a tour of one of these

recycling enterprises is an educational and amusing experience.

One of the most visible and best publicized manifestations of architectural decoration has been the emergence of the Post-Modernist style of architecture and design. At their best, Post-Modern buildings represent a deft blend of practical space planning of the International Style with such historically inspired details as cornices and moldings. In most cases, these details are not literal representations of those from the past. Instead, they are overscaled, twisted, or otherwise skewed to impart a sense of whimsy.

At the same time, a small but influential group of architects, designers, and homeowners are specifying details of an entirely different sort. Intended for specific spaces, these details are custom made by dedicated craftspeople in a variety of media. These people are linked to both the fine and applied arts. The handcraftsmanship they embody places them firmly in the tradition of the Arts and Crafts Movement. They have not rejected the machine, however, but use it to its best advantage in much the same way as Frank Lloyd Wright and International Style designers have done. They are the core of a tradition that has emerged as a serious field of study only in the past decade: that of architectural crafts.

Contemporary craftspeople are using historic techniques—and in some cases, original tools—to make details that are entirely new. The ancient craft of lead-

ed glass, for example, and the improvements initiated by Louis Comfort Tiffany are being combined to make unabashedly contemporary windows and transoms. Entirely new materials, some of which were developed for commercial purposes, are being fabricated with centuries-old techniques into *avant-garde* light fixtures and other items for the home.

Contemporary handcrafted architectural details are the focus of *Architectural Ornamentalism*. Although a number of the details shown in this book are rooted in historic influences, all examples are of contemporary vintage. None of them is located in historic shrines. Instead, they represent the state of the art of the serious, modern crafts movement. Most of them were found and photographed by Robert Perron during the past two years. *Architectural Ornamentalism* shows architectural details that blend seamlessly with their environment as well as fulfill their practical and aesthetic functions. Some of the details shown, such as the portfolios of stairways, gates, and window grilles, are eminently practical. Others, such as the fireplace mantels, rugs, and floorcloths, are more ornamental. Still other details are both, including the selection of interesting window treatments and striking light fixtures. In addition, information is included on the materials used and highlights of the elements' transformation from a raw state to fine finishing. Many of the individual artisans also describe their varied approaches to design and materials.

CHAPTER ONE

DETAILS THAT MAKE
A HOUSE COME ALIVE

*A structure gains character and interest when it is
imbued with detailing. The carved wooden door,
overhead rough-hewn beams, and ceramic inset shelf in
this house designed by Fischer-Smith & Associates
show a reliance on details from top to bottom.*

Round, hand-peeled spruce vigas are grouped in a visually engaging pattern on the ceiling of a circular bedroom, above. Above the logs, thin strips of wood called latillas are arranged in rhythmic herringbone fashion.

Details give architecture much of its personality and visual interest. In the past, they were integral parts of historic architectural styles that, in many cases, enabled the viewer to differentiate one from another. To cite only one example, it is the differences in the number and configuration of porch columns that help identify the various Victorian house styles of San Francisco.

Today, as the agitated waters of architectural style rush one way then another, details are enjoying a renewed celebrity as they are woven into the fabric of many disparate house styles.

Details can be small touches, such as an interesting ceiling treatment or a particular floor tile. Larger details can range from built-in storage to elements that define interior living areas. On one level, they can be viewed as simple embellishment to engage the eye, like displays of exterior Christmas lights, or as metaphors of history, like made-up coats of arms. On another level, however, contemporary architectural details fulfill genuine needs. Particular window shapes, for example, can work to shower the interior of a solar house with heat-generating light or to artfully frame a view, giving a sense of expansiveness to a small house.

In a tract or mass-designed house, details create what the architecture cannot—a sense of time and place. Regardless of the type of building style, they contribute the personal feel of the owners' outlook and even history and give a house an aura of its own.

In this chapter are two very different houses alive with architectural detailing. In one, the house shown on this page, details reinforce the traditionally inspired architecture. In the other, shown later in this chapter, they soften the stark, contemporary lines and imbue the house with a unique, multilayered character.

Located in Santa Fe, New Mexico, the first house is part of a newly developed residential condominium complex set on three rolling acres. All the houses in the complex, designed by Fischer-Smith & Associates, are firmly rooted in the Southwest building tradition and reflect the region's rich blend of Indian, Spanish, and Anglo architectural elements. But instead of merely reproducing the old, architectural designer Mike Fischer and his partner, Ron Smith, spiced the old with the flair and convenience of the new.

The emphasis on architectural detailing is established at the entry, where the ceiling soars upward, leaving exposed timbers called vigas, opposite below. The term *viga* refers to any hand-peeled, round timbers that supply primary structural support in an adobe house. These measure 11 inches in diameter and are made of spruce.

In the days of the frontier, vigas were built to support 12 to 18 inches of earth that served as the roof. "Before we had roofing compounds and hot tar out here," Fischer says, "we just put earth on the roof and graded it to allow rain to run off."

The vigas are illuminated by a modern element—a large, fixed skylight. A frame of weathered wood recycled from an old barn blends the contemporary glazing with the regionally inspired architecture. The vigas punctuate the interior walls, which are composed of plaster painted a pure "Navajo" white in keeping with the building tradition of the Southwest. The wall behind a console table is exposed adobe brick. The edges of the bricks have been wetted down, creating a thin layer of mud that visually softens this historic building material.

Because the architecture of the Southwest has historically used Spanish motifs and materials, the floor is covered by 12-by-12-inch ceramic tiles from Mexico.

The large, structural details are supplemented by small ones. Adjacent to the front door is a niche, or nicho, where the owners display a portion of their extensive handicrafts collection on a series of shelves 14 inches deep. The expanse of ceramic tile on the floor is broken up visually by the application of locally made decorative insets measuring 8 by 8 inches.

In the "kiva" bedroom, named because of its unusual

A circular design enlivens a guest bedroom, left, where the fireplace is set into the wall and a window is deftly placed to overlook a local ski area. The dresser is constructed of recycled wood from an old barn. In the foyer, vigas attract the eye upward to a sloped ceiling and a contemporary fixed skylight, below. A single adobe wall contrasts with the pure "Navajo" white of the traditional plaster walls. The floor is covered with Mexican ceramic tile enlivened with decorative insets manufactured in Santa Fe.

round shape, a built-in fireplace is set flush against the wall so that it does not protude into and visually dominate the room. The domelike shape of the fireplace opening, which measures 22 inches high by 21 inches wide, is a historic Southwest motif. A purely modern touch is the placement of the window, which is arranged to take advantage of the northerly view of the ski trails threading the Santa Fe ski basin. Another contemporary attitude is evident in the built-in dresser made of recycled barnwood, and the large wood closet.

The single most noticeable aspect of the room, however, is certainly the ceiling design of vigas made from Engelman spruce, top. Above the vigas are small branches, called latillas, set in a herringbone pattern. Though latillas can be made from many kinds of wood, among them cedar, fir, and oak, these particular ones are aspen. The built-up arrangement and visual interplay of the vigas and latillas extend toward the center from the wall, creating a domed appearance. Unlike many ceilings, this one is not embellished in any way. The only treatment that has been applied is a coat of oil.

This sort of exquisite detailing extends throughout the 2,700 square feet of living space. In the living area, for example, Fischer designed the fireplace to accommodate a favorite Indian pot belonging to the owners. Two additional niches hold collections of Casas Grandes pots as well as contemporary handicrafts.

Except for the Mexican ceramic tile in the entry, the rest of the flooring on the ground level is brick with radiant heating coils underneath. This system is supplemented by passive solar heat harvested by large, south-facing windows. Openings on the north side of the house are kept small to protect the interior from cold weather. But to keep the house from seeming claustrophobic, they are sensitively sited to wash the interior with constant northern light and capture views of the local ski area.

An expanse of shelving made of barnwood is both decorative and practical by providing space for collectibles, above. A plaster range hood lined with tile becomes the focal point in the traditionally designed but up-to-date kitchen, below.

Storage space assumes an artistic air in the study, where an expansive wall unit made of barnwood provides plenty of space to display an array of Southwestern handicrafts, left. The open shelving is designed in an L shape and measures 25 feet long. The wall unit, which was made by cabinetmaker Bob Richardson of Santa Fe, also incorporates a wet bar and low refrigerator for easy entertaining. It is supplemented by a shelf of ceramic tile imported from Mexico. On this expanse is a collection of native kachina dolls, books, pottery bowls, plants, and Indian art.

The shelving is visually broken up by a pair of leaded-glass panels by Santa Fe artist Catherine Bean. As in the foyer, the ceiling of the study is a delightful mix of traditional vigas and latillas with a modern skylight that gently illuminates the room with softly filtered light.

In keeping with the contemporary open floor plan of the entire house, the study is designed as a loft. On one side, it overlooks the foyer; on the other, the view is toward the living area.

The kitchen is visually anchored by a 4-foot-wide range hood sculpted from plaster, opposite below. Though it is designed in a traditional Southwestern shape, it incorporates a modern range hood and a ventilation fan that exhausts cooking odors to the outdoors.

The range hood is embellished with small, 4-by-4-inch Mexican ceramic tiles, forming a decorative "frieze." They are also repeated inside the hood as an easy-to-clean lining. The tile extends down to the counter tops and along the wall as a backsplash.

Flanking the range hood are two additional leaded-glass windows by Bean. These windows have an abstract floral motif that echoes the colors and motifs of the decorative tile. They are set into pine frames to contrast with the extensive application of plaster on the range hood and the walls.

All cabinetry in the kitchen is composed of red oak. It forms both the paneling on the refrigerator wall and the counters that wrap around the room, increasing the size of the workspace. In addition, the counter defines spaces by separating the kitchen from the dining area. There it becomes a convenient serving surface. An extension of the counter is topped with a copper inlay that provides a built-in pad on which to place hot dishes. The use of copper is repeated in a small bar sink set into the counter near the cooktop. It supplements the standard-size kitchen sink.

A large, fixed skylight above the exposed vigas brightens the kitchen work area.

To connect the first and second floors of the house, Fischer designed a stairwell leading from the foyer up to a catwalk corridor. In the spiral stairwell, the treads are made of 4-by-18-inch planks. The risers have been trimmed with brass.

One of the more interesting aspects of the stairwell are the custom-cast bronze handrails. These were made by a Sante Fe sculptor. Because the wall is a fairly irregular curve, the artist brought the molds to the construction site and bent them to conform to the contours of the surface. The molds were spined with wood and tape to secure them in the proper position and placed in an ice cooler for additional safety on the trip back to the artist's studio. There, the molds were placed in plaster and then cast in metal.

Custom-cast bronze railings sculpted by a local artist follow the curving contours of the wall surrounding a spiral staircase connecting the first and second floors, above. The treads are made of planks, while the risers are trimmed with brass.

Traditional details are evident on the exterior where a zaguan connects the two wings, left. Vigas penetrate the exterior walls above overhangs that shield the large windows from summer sun. In winter, bright sunlight supplies solar warmth. Extra heat is absorbed by the 10-inch-thick adobe walls.

A vaulted ceiling is clad with ceramic tile, creating a jewel of architectural detail in a small space, above. The hall leads to the round kiva bedroom.

A generous application of tile creates an entirely different effect in the master bathroom, left. The L-shaped whirlpool tub is built for two.

Because ceramic tile is a continually cool surface in a hot, arid climate, it has historically been a favored building material in the Southwest. Although tile abounds in this house, nowhere is it more dominant than in the master bathroom, opposite below left. This tile was manufactured in Talavera, Mexico, and handcut on the site to follow the contours of the curving steps and tub.

The tile on the wall is trimmed with 2-by-2-inch ceramic squares that are also used to outline the steps and the tub surround. These have a small geometric pattern. The expanse of wall tile is highlighted by a similar pattern on a much larger scale.

The application of tile is so pervasive in this room that it was also selected as the lining of the tub. It is designed in an L shape and is large enough to accommodate two people. A custom design by architect Michael Fischer, the whirlpool tub was handsculpted out of plastered concrete. During fabrication, the whirlpool outlets were imbedded into the structure. This inviting amenity was given a finishing flair of brass-plated fittings.

To the left is a shower stall and a steam room. At the rear is a leaded-glass window with an aspen leaf design. The pane is fitted into a standard casement window manufactured by Pella. When the owners open the window, they soak up the view of the ski slopes.

Even small areas of the house receive the same attention to detailing as the large ones. An excellent example is a short, vaulted hallway, opposite right. It leads to the kiva bedroom pictured on the preceding pages.

Although infrequently found in the architecture of New Mexico, the vault is part of the architecture of the region. Indigenous to the Middle East, it was transported by the Moors to Spain. From there, Spanish explorers exported it to the New World.

In this instance, however, the vault relates more to the curves of the kiva bedroom than to a historical precedence. The curve of the ceiling and the door at the end of the hall serve as a sympathetic introduction to those in the room. "Adobe lends itself to making curves for walls and even ceilings such as this one," Fischer says. "The curves make for an intriguing flow of space and extremely expressive walls." The visual effect is not one of the harshness sometimes associated with interior walls, but, instead, one of an undulating softness.

The ceiling itself is composed of Mexican tile over reinforced plaster. It hovers above a brick floor. The door is of weathered barnwood surrounded by a pine frame. Willow shutters conceal an opening in the wall, which is a pass-through to the kitchen.

Viewed from the exterior, the house blends seamlessly with its Southwestern surroundings, opposite above. The structure is sited so that it faces south. This enables the large windows to soak up both the panoramic views of Santa Fe and the sunlight for solar heating. In summer, the interior is shaded from solar gain by large overhangs.

The structure consists of two south-facing wings connected by a center section. At the very front of the house, the two wings are connected by an open corridor called a zaguan. On the left, it opens into the living area; to the right, the master bedroom.

The blockish architecture indigenous to the region is achieved by building the exterior walls 10 inches thick, the standard for a one-story adobe house. Two-story adobe houses are generally constructed with 14-inch-thick walls. For added architectural interest in keeping with the building tradition of the region, vigas penetrate the exterior walls.

The entry courtyard is paved with native flagstone in a reddish tone. The stones extend out to a brook that defines the property. This forms a much more pleasing naturalistic barrier, the designers feel, than that presented by an artificial wall or fence.

Only in recent years has detailing or ornamentation been incorporated into modern architecture. One of the most successful blendings of the two is this house, a sprawling 7,000-square-foot dwelling located in Connecticut. Designed by the architectural firm of Mackall and Dickinson, the house is visually alive with elegant details that not only create an intriguing sense of ornamentation but also make it highly functional.

The entry is separated from the living area by a change in floor level and materials and by a sleekly curved bookcase, above. Measuring 14 feet across by 9 feet deep, the bookcase provides a 48-foot expanse of storage space on two shelves in the entry. Because of the change in floor level between the two interior spaces, the bookcase is 3 feet high in the entry and 4½ feet tall in the living area. There, the inside of the curve incorporates a banquette that serves as the occupants' primary seating unit on the living area side.

This bookcase, however, carries out functions beyond storage and seating. As a space divider, it provides a distinct separation, yet it is low enough to allow a view through the interior from the front of the house to the back. "It makes the interior look quite light and bright," says architect Louis Mackall. "The level change simply puts back some of the intimacy and some of the privacy you would normally have with a separate entrance hall."

Constructed of white oak, the bookcase is defined at each end by supporting columns that reach up to the ceiling structure. The shelving is composed of solid wood strips that have been bent rather than sawn to fit the curve. On the top, smoked glass panels separate a series of wood "ribs" that radiate outward, emphasizing the circular nature of the curve, right. In addition, the open shelving, glass, and wood ribbing imbue the bookcase with an aura of transparency. Mackall says, "If you look at it long enough, you can understand all the pieces, how the bookcase was made; in short, what does what."

A secondary set of ribs extends out into the structure from each support column, above. At the same time, an edge piece extends beyond the column.

The entry is subtly separated from the living area in a contemporary Connecticut house by a sweeping, curved bookcase, upper left. On the top, wood ribs radiate outward, emphasizing the circular nature of the design, left. Additional ribbing unites the bookcase with timbers that define each end, above.

In the kitchen, right, exotic woods are woven into beautiful cabinetry including tall pantry units and a 10-foot-long work peninsula. Smoke and cooking odors from the restaurant stove are exhausted through a large copper hood that soars up 20 feet through the adjacent family area, below. Here, the large expanse of wall is punctuated by a cutout that provides an interior view of the two-story family area from a bedroom. The peaked hallway leads back to the second-floor bedrooms.

The peaked ceiling in the hallway is given a sense of transparency through the use of glass that forms an angled skylight, above. The glazing admits constant northern light, which flows into the bedrooms and balances light from the south-facing bedroom windows when the doors are left open.

Here, the large expanse of wall is punctuated by a cutout that provides an interior view of the two-story family area from a bedroom. The peaked hallway leads back to the second-floor bedrooms.

In the kitchen, opposite above, a number of woods have been sympathetically combined to create elegant cabinetry. A 10-foot-long peninsula containing the kitchen sink is made of teak with holly inlay. To the rear, the pantry is composed of tall cabinets of ash clapboard with teak framing on the front of each door. The floor is Mexican ceramic tile.

The kitchen work area enjoys an expanse of glazing exposing a southern view. In the other direction, a partial wall behind the commercial stove separates the kitchen from the family area. To ventilate cooking odors and create a strong vertical element in the family area, the architects designed a custom range hood that soars up two stories, opposite below left. Fabricated from copper, the hood measures 5 feet wide, 32 inches deep, and approximately 20 feet high.

"We try to make spaces that have a vertical aspect to them," says Connecticut craftsman Louis Mackall. "In this case, we combined the existing high space and the need to ventilate smoke from the stove. The height of the flue makes the hood draw better and reinforces the height of the family area."

The family area contains a dining area and entertaining space. It is overlooked by the second-floor hallway as well as a bedroom, which has a view down to the first floor through a cutout. In addition, the opening breaks up the expanse of wall behind the range hood, while crossbeams accent the lateral dimensions of the double-height space. Because the ceiling is so high, it was clad with 1-by-4-inch tongue-and-groove cedar. This design strategy visually warms the family area.

Although unintended, the cedar also emphasizes the peak shape of the ceiling, a motif that reappears throughout the house in the family-area cabinetry, the living-area fireplace, and the second-floor hallway leading to the bedrooms. The use of the peak motif, which most viewers would associate with the sense of rising, stems from Mackall's desire in his architecture to "encourage aspects of ascendancy. It's a spiritual endeavor."

A dark and dull atmosphere is often associated with such connectors as hallways. So half the ceiling peak in the corridor that leads back to the second-floor bedrooms is topped with an angled skylight, opposite right. Besides being an intriguing detail, the skylight is a practical source of daylighting. It also enables natural light to filter into the bedrooms when the doors are open, which balances the illumination that is gained through the south-facing windows during the day.

The peak motif recurs in the dining room window, where it is incorporated into a fanciful rendition of a bay window, right. The purpose of the 9-foot-high window is to illuminate the upper portion of the room. The design

In the dining area, an avant-garde bay window ushers light indoors, above.

is also an attempt to extend the traditional bay window upward as well as out into the landscape. Or as Mackall describes it, "I wanted to make a bay window that looked as though one had taken a cherry bomb and exploded it in the wall so that the bay went out in all directions."

The north wall of the house is composed of old bricks recycled from a Brooklyn demolition site, right. Instead of being laid flat, the bricks are arranged diagonally to form peaks.

Peaked windows inserted in the clapboard siding on the south-facing wall usher sunlight and solar heat indoors, below.

Though fine carpentry and an elegant sense of joinery abound throughout the house, they are most evident in the entry and living area, opposite above. The curving bookcase pictured on the preceding pages sweeps around the space to meet a built-in bar at one end. At the other end, it leads to a step down into the living area. The inner area of this unusual bookcase is an expansive banquette.

In the entry, the front door is a deft blend of the solidity of wood and the transparency of glass, opposite below. The entry is visually lightened by a section of glazing that soars upward toward the ceiling. The peak motif that appears so frequently in the house is first introduced beside the door. In this case the peak, which contains a panel of light switches, consists of drywall framed in wood.

"What one is doing when designing a front door is often two contradictory things," says architect Mackall. "While you're trying to invite people in, which is accomplished here by using glass, at the same time you're trying to keep people out for the sake of privacy, enclosure, and safety."

Here's how the idea of a "welcoming barrier" is seen from the outdoors, left. First, in the upper portion of the entry are pieces of glass so small "that one literally could not crawl through them," says Mackall. The glazing in the lower area is large enough to ensure a view and create "an invitation" to come indoors. Softening the visual impact of the house is old brick that was recycled from a demolition site in Brooklyn, New York. It is set diagonally, creating peaks and valleys on the north wall of the house.

From the south, the expanse of oiled cedar clapboard siding is broken up by a series of peaked windows on the first floor and large rectangular openings on the second. These harvest winter sunlight to heat the interior through direct solar gain.

Along the east wall is a shed extension containing the master bath. As for the style of the architecture, Mackall says, "When we started and I asked the owners what they liked, they answered a chalet they visited in Switzerland. So that's where I started, even though it's obviously not a literal representation." However, a hint of the Swiss genesis of the architecture can be seen on the east wall in the series of peaked roofs.

In the living area, above, the bookcase sweeps around to become an expanse of banquette seating. On the upper level is the entry, which is paved with Mexican tile. In the living area, the floor treatment changes to wood.

A front door designed by Mackall serves as a "welcoming barrier" in the entry, below. The obvious architectural contradiction is achieved by combining the solidity of wood with the transparency of glass.

CHAPTER TWO

DETAILING WITH WOOD

This striking unit by Ed Zucca combines a soaring brick fireplace, a traditional mantel, and a wealth of storage space, illustrating how wood detailing can bring a great sense of individuality, warmth, and comfort to a room.

Probably no material used in architecture has the comparable warmth, appeal, and practicality of wood. In houses both old and new, wood is everywhere. Along with brick and stone it is one of the basic building blocks for structural elements forming foundations, columns, roofs, and decks. Indoors wood is omnipresent. It clads walls, ceilings, and floors and is fashioned into a range of furnishings.

The tradition of building with wood existed before recorded history. For centuries wood was the primary source of fuel and power. Eventually it was hacked into crude tables and chairs. Although they were progressively refined, some basic designs, such as the tavern table, still exist as a modern furnishing option. Seventeenth- and eighteenth-century master carvers crafted wood into exquisite, functional furnishings that have proved to be of lasting interest. The early machine age left its imprint on wood, too, as it was steamed, bent, twisted, and glued into fanciful shapes.

Twentieth-century wood furnishings faced stiff competition from the emerging preference for metal as a design choice. Wood has been rivaled as a building material by the technological development of many materials, among them aluminum, vinyl, and plastic laminates. Today the role of wood as an architectural mainstay faces challenges from new resins and acrylics. Although durable and resilient, none of these materials match the enduring appeal and versatility of honest-to-goodness wood. In the proper hands the inherent beauty and practicality of wood can be crafted into fine details admirably suited for contemporary living. One of the most exciting forefronts of the rediscovery of wood is the arena of architectural crafts. Wood details are being

incorporated into the fabric of a house, not just in terms of structure, but as useful and visually pleasing design elements.

There are some excellent and inspiring examples of modern woodworking in this chapter. Some are unabashedly contemporary, others are *avant-garde*, and still others continue traditional forms. All of them, however, share two common traits. First, each is appropriate in its architectural and design context and second, each represents the very highest quality of craftsmanship in its execution.

Used sensitively, wood is appropriate for any room in today's home. Wood is, of course, no stranger to the kitchen. But where many unimaginative architects specify plain, painted-over-wood carpentry, architect William Lipsey designed a kitchen in Aspen, Colorado, that lets wood and craftsmanship speak for themselves, opposite.

He gave great thought to the everyday tasks of preparing and storing food. Because the pantry had to be fitted into a narrow space, the architect designed it so that it curves out, increasing storage space, above. On the doors, the contrasting framework draws attention to the vertical carving. The curve of the pantry is echoed by the overhead cabinetry in the work area. Here the wood is relieved by glass cabinet doors, generous applications of ceramic tile, and the transparency created by a pass-through into the adjacent eating area.

The kitchen pantry, a common storage element, above, takes on a sculptural air by curving outward in a house designed by architect William Lipsey.

The curve from the kitchen pantry repeats in the crown of the upper cabinetry in the work area, creating a pleasing, cohesive design.

Awash with light, this airy
kitchen by architect Louis
Mackall deftly blends etched
glass and light-toned wood,
above. In this inviting
environment, the focal point is
a copper ventilating stove hood,
whose intriguing curves are
reminiscent of sculpture.

At one end, the peninsula
becomes a round dining surface
cut flat to permit circulation
into the work area, right.

In this kitchen design by Louis Mackall, the hood for the gas stove becomes the focal point of the room. Instead of the bleak commercial eyesore of sleek stainless steel one might expect, this hood is made of copper, which is aging to a lovely soft patina.

The ventilation hood and the peninsula mark the upper boundary between the work area and the adjoining space. This design approach eschews overhead cabinetry As a result, the view from the work area is preserved.

Storage space abounds in this work area. Along the rear, the appliance wall is an expanse of wood-framed cabinetry in light tones, below. Located both above and below the work counter, the doors are fitted with frosted glass that reinforces the feeling of airiness in the space, but obscures the view of the contents of the cabinetry.

The pensinsula is a remarkable bit of kitchen detailing. On the work side, it incorporates low storage for pots and pans. On the opposite side are a low counter for informal meals and shelving. There is even a drawer with an etched-glass front included.

At one end, the peninsula becomes a second dining surface, lower left. The table surface becomes flat on the work area side so movement into the space is not impeded. The peninsula includes a convenient panel of lighting controls and an electrical outlet, enabling the work area to be expanded onto the table surface when large meals are being prepared. For entertaining, the table can be used as a secondary serving area. The lovely wood detailing is shown to the right.

An interesting detail of the dining/serving table, above, is its widow's peak corner. The fine etching of the angular lines bordering the corner defines the homey warmth of the wood.

Placing the cabinetry on the appliance wall, left, enlarges the visual space and permits the cook to be in the center of things rather than off in a corner. The tones of the modern appliances blend gracefully with the delicate wood, the glass, the weathered copper of the hood, and the antique copper and pewter cooking utensils.

Designing a kitchen that is elegant in its simplicity and yet canny in its use of space is a challenge. All too often a kitchen may become a showcase for futuristic designs or kitsch. Keeping within dimensions while letting the materials and qualities of the kitchens speak for themselves is a feat that architects Randall Mudge and Tage Frid have been able to successfully accomplish.

In designing the kitchen of a New Hampshire home, below, Randall Mudge employed the current fashion of blending white and wood tones in a dramatic way. Instead of harmonizing light wood and muted white, he chose rich, saturated wood tones and created a strong sense of contrast with the bright white of the walls, appliances, and lighting fixtures. Wood is everywhere in

this kitchen, from the below-counter storage space and the window frames to the exposed joists overhead.

Simple and practical, the work area is defined by an extension, which contains the cooktop. Storage is available on both sides so that pots and pans can be kept concealed in the work area, while linens and dining accessories can be stored on the other. The overhead cabinetry is lightened visually by glass doors, which help

The rustic appeal of this kitchen, created by Randall Mudge, is refined by the urbane, highly reflective marble work surface, below. The warm tones of the wood are reinforced by the use of contrasting white on the walls, appliances, and light fixtures.

the cook, or any first-time guests who would like to help set the table, find the objects that they need at a glance.

While the overall impression is rustic and casual, the kitchen is made truly elegant by the addition of a marble countertop. The marble has a highly reflective finish, which is much richer, more urbane, and more visually arresting than the mundane option of ceramic tiles. Suspended light fixtures, spare and informal enough for a country kitchen, provide an abundance of task lighting and eliminate the need for fluorescent fixtures.

Sometimes the space designed for a kitchen, particularly in older houses, is basically a glorified hallway. Tage Frid tackled this difficult design dilemma in a Connecticut Colonial home undergoing serious renovation. He distracted attention from the narrow shotgun-like space by designing cabinetry in economical and innovative shapes, above and right. This series of cabinets stretches right up to the ceiling, employing the maximum vertical space. The uppermost cabinets are equipped with sliding wooden doors. These cabinets are arranged to store less frequently needed items, such as chafing dishes and the serving platter used only at Thanksgiving.

Below these are intriguing storage-space cabinets that open up instead of out. In fact, their design is reminiscent of a wooden version of the appliance hood. Instead of hiding blenders and toasters, this cabinetry keeps glassware and everyday dishes at a very accessible level. To open, the owners pull up the handles from the bottom and the wooden door set on tracks recesses into the top.

The appearance of separate wood strips on the doors of the storage cabinetry designed by Tage Frid, top, is simulated by a tambour finish on the exterior side of the work peninsulas, which are set at each end of the work area, above. The storage cabinets, reminiscent of wooden appliance hoods, open from the bottom.

To complement the wooden cabinets both peninsulas have a tambour finishing. While the work area is aluminum, the peninsulas have wooden surfaces. The earthy color of the tiles used for the floor harmonize with the warm tones of the wood cabinetry. The work and serving counters can also double as dining surfaces.

What at first view appears to be a small extension of the kitchen counter is, on closer inspection, a highly practical wood detail, right. For in addition to storing utensils and supplying supplemental work space, this inventive "extension" is actually portable, below. Admirably suited to a small kitchen, the cart, when moved, forms an island or is rolled to the table for carving meats and serving salads and desserts. Its deceptive appearance of permanence is achieved by the insets that enable the cart to be set over the steps leading from the kitchen to a hallway.

Seamless design and portability combine harmoniously in this small kitchen, above. Designed by Ronald Phipps, the work area is defined by a compact, movable extension which also serves as a work space and space divider, left.

While the extension is perfectly fitted to accommodate a short series of steps, it actually rolls out and opens to become a portable work counter and serving cart. The lower portion provides storage space, while the top is a compact work surface with a compartment to hold knives and other work utensils. Set on concealed casters, the extension can roll out from the peninsula position to become an island that may be placed in the center of the room for additional separation between the work and dining areas. Then, when needed, this small detail can be moved to the dining table as a sort of sideboard.

Beauty and function also combine in artisan Dale Broholm's work. In this rare kitchen that soars up to the roof peak, below, elements of old and new are blended. The kitchen includes exposed beams with an old-fashioned flavor yet has track lighting running across the beams, as well as a clearly modern skylight. Cutouts in the wall are used in a thoroughly modern manner to facilitate the circulation of light and air to the upper portion of the house.

This kitchen is also unusual in the way it has been brought directly into the public zone of the house, rather than being tucked away in a less visible area. Here, by recognition of the fact that the kitchen is a heavily used communal area, the room has been made a focal point with its sleek surfaces, uniquely shaped furnishings, and a contrasting color scheme.

Glossy surfaces adorn Broholm's built-in units on the appliance wall and on the suspended cabinetry. The sleek approach continues on the contemporary, U-shaped work counter, as well as on the seating units,

which are unusually designed and very comfortable.

With low backs and high seats, these units are essentially stools that enable family members to use the work counter as a dining surface and allow dinner guests to visit with the cook during meal preparation. The tops and bottoms of the chairs are identical. At the top is a curved back. At the floor, Broholm incorporated rounded feet and at the back wooden connecting strips called stretchers that vary in shape. At the front is a practical footrest.

Each unit asserts its individuality, especially in the middle of each. Here the legginess of the piece is rendered in the form of zig-zags or severely pointed angles. Visually emphasizing these forms is an array of colors, from black to red—which carries through the palette of the work counter—to shades of blue and lavender.

Shown at left is a kitchen with furniture and built-in units by Dale Broholm. Visually appealing as well as comfortable, these avant-garde stools gracefully combine form and function.

Most people would immediately reject the idea of an all-wood kitchen. But because woodworking is craftsman Tommy Simpson's specialty, the material was a natural choice in building his own kitchen, opposite.

The almost exclusive application of wood in this setting is entirely appropriate, for this kitchen is located in an old farmhouse that has been sensitively remodeled by Simpson and his wife, fiber craftswoman Missy Stevens. The wood detailing echoes the material and decorative atmosphere of the exposed timbers and ceiling overhead.

Except for the etched-glass door inserts in the cabinetry and the kitchen sink, all surfaces in this appealing kitchen are either made of wood or clad with it. Of course, the casual visitor would expect to see wood used for the cabinetry and for the floor.

What is not so common these days is the use of wood for other elements. Here the material is used for the cabinet handles, work surface, backsplash, and even as a decorative treatment for the refrigerator and freezer doors, which sport intriguingly curved wood handles.

Although evocative of the old and rustic, the kitchen is an excellent example of modern kitchen design because at its center is a work triangle. Along the wall shown in the photograph is the modern full-size refrigerator. Next to it are a sink and the upper and lower cabinetry. All of these work to establish the triangle because of the way they are placed and, in turn, the way the owner moves from one to another.

The seamless design quality established by the use of wood belies the compact size of the kitchen. In fact, the only element that reveals the shallowness of this storage and work area is the placement of the sink faucet, which is set to the side rather that at the back.

At the top of the room is an etched-glass clerestory window, through which light flows into the small space from the adjacent dining area. Below that is the upper cabinetry. Here, too, etched glass was specified to lighten the extensive application of wood. The lower cabinetry includes a stacked row of drawers as well as two smaller drawers containing specialty cooking utensils. Completing the third position of the triangle is the placement of the cooktop and oven on the opposite wall.

By setting the hot portions of the kitchen away from the refrigerator, Simpson ensured that the oven or cooktop would not make the refrigerator work overtime.

Establishing the perfect tone for the entire kitchen is the oak floor, the most common of surface treatments. While wooden floors in kitchens practically disappeared following the advent of tile and synthetic coverings, they have enjoyed a renaissance of sorts in recent years. Part of the reason for the resurgence of the wood kitchen floor lies in the development of durable, yet easy-care, protective finishes such as polyurethane.

Because Simpson extended the wood floor into the kitchen from the rest of the house, the sense of separation of the food preparation area and the main body of the interior is lessened. This sort of development has been appreciated by many a homeowner who no longer needs to feel that the one who cooks has been shut off from everybody else. This design approach is also appreciated by many guests who like to visit with the cook in the kitchen, no matter how cramped it is.

Recognizing that people will want to gather in the kitchen, Stevens decorated the floor with a welcome mat of sorts. It is a rug handmade by Stevens, whose artistry is documented in the chapter on fiber on pages 126 and 127. This area rug is embellished with four birds and subdued, multicolored striping.

From the oak floor to the exposed ceiling, wood has been deftly incorporated into the kitchen by owners and craftpeople Tommy Simpson and Missy Stevens, opposite. The simple and seemingly rustic ambience, however, does not disguise the thoughtful space planning that went into the design.

In a house designed by architect Robert Knight, the staircase becomes a work of art, left. From the center support beam the treads and banister radiate out in a spiral, above.

Some of the most difficult spaces to infuse with a sense of contemporary elegance and pizazz are connectors, such as foyers and hallways. These are important because they introduce visitors to, and ease their movement through, an interior. Modern houses are usually compact, and space has to be dealt with economically and reserved for practical use. In older houses, of course, this was not the case. Older houses often radiate out from a large, gracious foyer and, both physically and visually, up through a grandly carved staircase. The foyers and stairways of Victorian houses were made visually riveting by the addition of stock gingerbread millwork.

The connectors of modern houses obviously do not lend themselves to the old approaches. Embellishments such as gingerbread millwork would make an already limited space seem even smaller. Less is more in a small space but, unfortunately, the choices are often uninspired. The alternative often seems relegated to a functional wood stairway or a stock metal spiral staircase.

But the work of craftspeople creates many innovative options that are aesthetically pleasing and can also be

Tapering balusters reinforce the lightness of the design while echoing the fine sense of detailing incorporated into this most practical and inviting of contemporary architectural elements, above.

personalized. Here is a portfolio of outstanding wood staircases that are not only practical and space-efficient but are also artful in their design and execution. Because these designs are custom installations, not all of them are suitable for every house. Each does show the creativity that the liberated mind can achieve—whether it belongs to an architect, designer, or craftsperson—and can serve as inspiration for other, personalized approaches.

The stairway illustrated on the opposite page is an excellent alternative to the spiral metal variety. When the owners of this home in Maine consulted architect Robert Knight, they agreed with him that they would make a serious investment in the staircase since it would be a dominant interior element and a visual focal point. This beautiful stairway is a collaboration between Knight and designer Scott Dickerson. Knight conceived of the setting and spatial proportions while Dickerson designed and built the stairway. Although Dickerson's work is usually confined to creating seating, such as sofas and chairs, he enjoyed accepting the challenge of this unusually interesting architectural project.

The house is 2,000 square feet and is solar- and wood-heated. The composition of the house revolves around a masonry chimney. The stairway, crafted of a yellow birch, one of the most abundant hardwoods of the Northeast, was set right next to the chimney. It literally curls around the main structural column, which is a combination of narrower planks laminated together, left. The beam provides support to the extent that traditional stringers or bridgeboards are not needed.

Incorporated into the supporting beam are three sharp angles, so that the stairway thrusts back, up, and forward into space. Although this design could easily have turned out to be harsh, it is not, primarily because of the lightness and delicacy of the entire structure. In fact, the sharp angularity of the beam provides a very nice contrast with the gently curving handrail and second-floor banister, left.

For added visual lightness, risers were eschewed and the treads arranged so that they radiate out from the main support beam. Delicately tapered balusters have been included to support the handrail, above.

A wood staircase, right, pulls double duty as a storage unit, with an abundance of space to keep toys and other necessities well out of sight on the lower level. It was designed by architect Harry Teague.

Above the storage unit, the staircase jettisons and its risers become a set of stairs that creates an atmosphere of transparency and lightness, below left. While most of this project is made of wood, the top step departs from the norm because it is made of metal, which is echoed by the handrail and balusters.

The two staircases featured on these pages are both space-efficient yet very graceful. Their attention to fine detailing makes them unique, each from a different perspective. One is contemporary, using traditional materials in an inventive way, and the other—with subtle deviations—is traditional.

The enticing stairway designed by Harry Teague, left and lower left, is the more contemporary of the two and bridges the gap between old and new forms. While it gives a nod to tradition by incorporating bridgeboards, treads, banisters, and balusters, each of these elements is rendered in a thoroughly modern fashion.

The most notable departure from tradition are the balusters and handrails, for which Teague specified metal instead of the wood one would expect. However, there is not scarcity of wood in this unique staircase. Wood abounds in this staircase, particularly in the base, which doubles as an expansive storage area with doors to conceal the clutter of everyday living.

The staircase design is a case study in the maximum use of limited space. Only a small amount of floor space is required for the base, but the impression of a grander staircase is created when is turns the corner at the bottom. In reality it shoots almost directly up to the next level of the house.

In the middle, the staircase moves beyond the built-in storage unit on the lower level and becomes merely a flight of stairs. While this is a small change, it dramatically alters the character of the unit by creating an openness that makes the upper portion seem almost transparent. At the same time this approach emphasizes the base and its rich wood tones.

To finish off the staircase, Teague added a bit of whimsy in the form of a metal step that is open like a grate. The owners have reinforced this light-hearted approach by "accessorizing" the entire storage-staircase unit with motifs reminiscent of small-space environments, such as a toy plane and a nautical clock.

In a more traditional vein, the roughhewn and the sleek have been artfully combined by craftsman Tommy Simpson in the staircase he designed for his own house, opposite right and below. Spanning several levels of the old farmhouse that he and his wife, fiber-artist Missy Stevens, painstakingly restored, the staircase is light and delicate in its design and fabrication. As such, it contrasts sharply with the rugged ceiling beams and the exposed floorboards of the level above.

Except for the handrail and newel post, which are stained dark, light tones are specified for the staircase structure. The lightness of the wooden floors and staircase and the white of the walls visually open up the space, while the darker handrail and newel post harmonize with the dark beams of the ceiling. The balusters are individually handcarved and embellished with a variety of motifs that give the wood a sculptural air, below. This attention to detailing imbues the staircase with the individuality that bespeaks the mark of fine craftsmanship and sensitivity to materials.

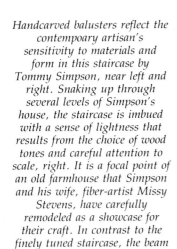

Handcarved balusters reflect the contempoary artisan's sensitivity to materials and form in this staircase by Tommy Simpson, near left and right. Snaking up through several levels of Simpson's house, the staircase is imbued with a sense of lightness that results from the choice of wood tones and careful attention to scale, right. It is a focal point of an old farmhouse that Simpson and his wife, fiber-artist Missy Stevens, have carefully remodeled as a showcase for their craft. In contrast to the finely tuned staircase, the beam overhead has been left in its original, roughhewn state.

A staircase bursting with imagery, this remarkable detail by craftsman Tom Luckey radically departs from tradition.

Most staircases are merely a set of steps inside a vertical space, very similar to an elevator shaft. Craftsman Tom Luckey took the idea of staircase-as-shaft and designed a set of stairs that are not only hauntingly evocative of a variety of natural phenomena but are also as much fun to climb as playground equipment. Every step up or down creates another overall perspective, and each new view will elicit a markedly different description.

The stairway is located in a contemporary house whose owners are connoisseurs of many other fine crafts. This example of beautiful craftsmanship occupies an area just the size of an elevator shaft, in fact, and shoots directly up to connect the two levels of the house. When viewed casually from the bottom, opposite, the stairs resemble a square of shelving recessed into the wall. The careful viewer, however, discerns an opening in the planes of wood that allows the owners to enter the stairway. This visual magic makes access to the staircase seem somehow especially exclusive.

In contrast, from the top the stairway opens in a pit-like fashion, above right . Here the exterior structure of the stairway shows series of squares that look as if they have been carved open with highly organic shapes to create the steps and necessary headroom required as one descends to the lower level. From a distance the entryway almost could be perceived as a flat wooden square

in which intricate patterns of varying depths have been carved. As one descends the steps and reaches the middle of the staircase, the real fun begins. Here the visual effect of the design is open to personal interpretation as the rich imagery stimulates the imagination. The delicately carved steps of wood could be ancient but well-defined layers of geological strata or, from a more irreverent point of view, they could be a sectional look at an enormous rib cage. The pale color of the wood and the graduating layers are also reminiscent of mushrooms that attach to the side of trees.

On close inspection one can see that each of the many steps is highly detailed. Most steps have carving on the top and some have it on the bottom. Large cutouts at the back of the steps create texture and lighten the visual effect by enabling light to filter up and down this unusual stairwell. Although the fine curves of the steps and their slender supports lend the project a delicate, even fragile, appearance, the steps are actually exceedingly sturdy. Firm connections to the wall are supplemented in the center by a number of small toothpicklike supports set at various strategic angles.

When viewed from the back in a hallway of the house, upper left, the steps are revealed to be flat and straight at the back, actually structuring the staircase and contributing to its stability.

*What appears to be a simple
stairway, above, in actuality
leads a double life. Designed by
Tom Luckey, a mechanism
beneath the structure converts it
into a slide.*

One of the features that homeowners miss when they opt for a contemporary staircase is the fun of sliding down the banister, since today's staircases often don't include this feature. Craftsman and designer Tom Luckey no doubt had this option in mind when he built this staircase that provides two methods of descent, left.

Most of the time the steps serve the utilitarian purpose of promoting circulation between the two floors of the house, right. To serve this purpose, the construction of the stairs appears to consist of bridgeboards and treads.

But the simple appearance of the staircase is deceptive. If the owners of the house are ever tempted to have some fun they might employ the staircase for its second use. Whenever it is needed or wanted, this stairway turns into a slide, right. The operating mechanism, consisting of pulleys and levers, is concealed on the underbelly of the stairway. When the mechanism is activated, the entire stairway shifts so that the treads line up in proper order and anyone can slide gracefully from one floor to another.

In addition, these simple steps are enlivened by carved forms, such as trees and abstract stick figures, that have a hieroglyphic feeling to them, below.

As evidenced by some of his other staircases, shown on pages 44 and 45, Tom Luckey is never satisfied with the obvious, nor limited by a sense of the expected. His abstract sense of humor and creative perspective make every staircase he designs an adventure. The artistry of this staircase/slide almost qualifies it as sculpture.

For a fast trip to the first floor, the owners merely activate a series of pulleys that shift the stair treads to create the slide, above. Besides reflecting a great sense of whimsy, the stair/slide also embodies artful carving on the bridgeboards, left.

The emphasis on the ''new geometry'' in architecture in the late 1970s and early 1980s led to some interesting interplay of shapes and forms on exteriors. That approach has been brought indoors and enlivened with a juxtaposition of disparate materials imaginatively used in these two staircases.

Tom Luckey's work, as shown on the preceding pages, is full of fun that in no way compromises function. Here the fun continues in a vertically oriented contemporary house. This fanciful stairway incorporates a series of calligraphic curves that defines the overall form as well as the detailing on one side, right. The stairs are made of richly grained wood cut in scimitar-shaped arcs. These are complemented by the embellishments on the handrails, which are cut from the same detailed wood. When the stairway is viewed from the second floor, looking down to the first, the massive solid railing that provides the stairway's main structural support is contrasted with a wonderfully airy openness on the opposite side, above.

The rounded handrail is supported by a series of delicate, slender balusters, which are interwoven with laminated pieces of wood that curve both up and out beyond the stairway. These curved pieces appear solid when looked down upon, but seem like fine floating curls when viewed from underneath. As an added fillip, risers have been eliminated even at the bottom so that the whole staircase seems to float in midair.

An airiness of a different sort has been achieved by architect Randall Mudge. He streamlined the stairs in

another contemporary house by jettisoning the handrails and balusters altogether, below. To emphasize the treads and risers, the bottom portion of the wall consists not of wood, as one might expect, but of wallboard. In this way the stairway divides the space without a loss of light and without creating a claustrophic feeling.

Similar tones of wood are used in the stairway, as well as on the ceiling, the balcony handrail for the next land-
ing, the curved window frames above, and in the distant kitchen cabinetry. These woods harmonize and coordinate all the areas into one large, organic space. To give this simple stair treatment added elegance, Mudge has made the last few steps at the bottom turn right rather than extending them straight down. The turn of the staircase ensures that the person descending it will make an impressive entrance.

A playful series of curves is deftly incorporated into this staircase by craftsman Tom Luckey, left. Beside forming the overall structure, curves embellish the treads and spaces between the balusters.

Angularity and openness are the keys to understanding this stairway by architect Randall Mudge, right. Here, the architect dispensed with handrails and layered the wood on the structure as an interesting surface treatment.

Above, a cherry-and-ash doorway by architect William Lipsey is set against a clapboard siding exterior, with a gymnasium light above it. The large transom illuminates the interior.

The owners of this delightful Colorado vacation house have their pick of several impressive doorways to enter. The secondary entrance, above, is part of a small extension that was later added to the original large house. "It's like a little building with a door in it," says the architect, William Lipsey.

A delightful juxtaposition of materials, the extension is framed with pine clapboard. In contrast with this rusticated version of Colonial American architecture is the elegance of the door materials, which are a blend of cherry-wood rails flanking ash paneling. Atop the door is a transom measuring approximately 3 feet high that adds a sense of importance to the doorway.

A final fillip is a basketball light with a metal mesh ball guard. "The idea was to create a sort of richness by combining a lot of diverse elements," says Lipsey. "It's elegant on one level; it says high school gymnasium on another; and it's sort of Western on yet another level."

Besides adding significance to the doorway, the transom is practical. It increases the amount of indoor light on the north-facing elevation. In addition, that light balances the light gained through a large picture window on the wall opposite the door.

The front door of the house also combines cherry and ash, but here the visual effect is quite different, right. Slightly wider than a conventional doorway, it measures 3½ feet wide. The door is framed by solid glass blocks set in a cherry-wood frame. The glazing repeats in the center of the door, which is punctuated by a large sheet of beveled glass. Incorporating glass into the entry has Colonial American overtones, but here, too, it has been interpreted in an unmistakably Western manner. "It's kind of like looking sideways over your shoulder at the past," says Lipsey.

Framed with glass, the front door of a Colorado vacation house elegantly blends cherry and ash woods, left. For an added sense of transparency, the door is punctuated by a large pane of beveled glass.

*A slightly curved top creates
an arch of wood in this
doorway, above.
The framing breaks
up the generous application
of siding in this entryway.*

For an architectural detail that is inherently rectangular in shape, doors can assume an amazing variety of forms. Consider the doors illustrated here. In a house brimming with natural materials, architect Eldred Mowery created a doorway with geometric decoration and contrasting woods, far right.

Geometric forms create a completely different effect for a front door designed by architect Harry Teague, below. Glass forms a triangle that extends in truncated form into a side panel. Complementing the glazing in the center is an expanse of highly polished metal.

Architect Ric Weinschenk adapted the historic generic form of a fanlight for the front door of a contemporary house. Instead of placing it above the door, he incorporated it directly into the wood itself, right, and split it in half so that one portion is on each double door.

In a house in Colorado, architect Harry Teague created an impressive entry and relieved the expanse of exterior wood siding with a door framed in wood, left. The center portion consists of a sheet of galvanized metal, a material reminiscent of the region's mining past.

*A staple of Colonial American
architecture—the fanlight—has
been reinterpreted and
incorporated into the door of
this new house by architect Ric
Weinschenk, above.*

*Geometry assumes an
intriguing air in this lovely
doorway, which illustrates a
blend of wood, glass, and
metal. The focal points of the
entry are large panes of glass.*

*Geometric detailing draws
visual attention to the doorway
of a contemporary house. In
this context, the wood blends
beautifully with the extensive
use of natural materials.*

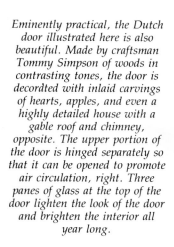

Eminently practical, the Dutch door illustrated here is also beautiful. Made by craftsman Tommy Simpson of woods in contrasting tones, the door is decordted with inlaid carvings of hearts, apples, and even a highly detailed house with a gable roof and chimney, opposite. The upper portion of the door is hinged separately so that it can be opened to promote air circulation, right. Three panes of glass at the top of the door lighten the look of the door and brighten the interior all year long.

It is sometimes forgotten that doors are called upon to perform a number of functions. Besides permitting circulation into and out of a house, they keep in small children and pets, keep out cold in winter, and serve as a primary means of ventilation in the summer. Doors are also a decorative ornament to a room and help define its style and character.

One of the oldest types of doors is the Dutch door. Reminiscent of the doors that have traditionally been built into barns, this variety consists of two hinged sections that can be opened independently or joined to open as a single unit.

In a house in Connecticut, craftsman Tommy Simpson has updated this historic genre with an exquisite example of the Dutch door that neatly unites practicality and artfulness. As a single unit, the door has the appearance of a modern entryway that has been spiced with historic overtones, opposite right. Dark woods form the frame of the door, which is fleshed out with

panels that have been made of contrasting light wood.

The door imaginatively incorporates subtle decorative carving of two light-wood hearts in both the upper and lower portions of the dark framing. The upper area has a darker apple motif. For contrast, the portions of light wood are decorated with stars carved from darker wood, and at the very bottom of the door is a highly detailed silhouette of a house that is complete with a historic gable roof and even a chimney.

The upper portion of the door is fitted with three panes of glass at the top that permit the owner to scrutinize arriving visitors. At the same time the glazing lightens the look of the door and brightens the interior of the house all year long.

In keeping with tradition, the upper portion of the door is hinged separately. This facilitates the free flow of hot air indoors in summer, heightens interior light levels, keeps small children and pets safely indoors, and provides an alternative and expanded view.

There must be an almost inexhaustible number of strategies for personalizing a house with architectural details. One of the most unusual ways is to incorporate carvings of the owners or other significant persons associated with the design and construction of the structure. This approach, of course, is not without historic precedence, as can be seen in the Woolworth Building in New York City and some of the mansions in Newport, Rhode Island.

Personalized carvings scaled to life size are rare and often unsettling, and these examples are large scale and monumental. Imagine the surprise of visitors to this house in Winston, North Carolina, when they open the door to find carved portraits staring at them, above.

The craftsman, Bob Trottman, chose to have three faces since there are three members of the household. The three faces are echoed again by the small ceramic faces hung to the left of the door. These are the work of ceramic artist Tom Suomalainen, also located in Winston, North Carolina.

Evenly placed in a vertical line, the visual effect is somewhat uncanny as the carvings are limited to facial features—eyes, nose, cheekbones, and mouth—with no attempt to include hair or ears. Adding to the striking

nature of the detail is the depth of the carving, which in the case of the eyes and mouth seems to extend completely through the door.

The faces are carved on a swinging door that connects the dining room and an adjacent pantry. To create the faces, Bob Trottman used three inner panels of Honduras mahogany. He carved the features from the middle panel, the thickest, and then blended the panel's edges in with the other panels. On the other side the door is flat, and the corresponding middle panel is recessed.

On a more practical front, the renewed emphasis on energy-efficient design in recent years has caused architects to have to cope with the problem of blending an old element—the air-lock entry—into contemporary design schemes. One of the more aesthetically successful of these is this entry, opposite, which was designed by architect George Buchanan.

To lighten the visual effect of the oak door, Buchanan designed it to include a great deal of glass. Besides the tall side panel, composed of leaded-glass panes by Kenneth von Roenn, the door is literally sliced into sections by carving that has been filled with thin strips of clear glazing. The rounded portion of the end of each strip has colored glass. The design of this door is repeated by the interior door, which can be easily seen through the side glass panel.

Operated in tandem, the doors enable the owners to enter the air-lock entry, close the outer door, then proceed through the inner door into the interior while minimizing the amount of heat loss in winter. In summer, the principle works in reverse to minimize the escape of cool interior air to the outdoors.

In further juxtaposition to the wood and glass, the floor of the foyer is covered with ceramic tile, adding to the interesting interplay of materials. In addition, the tile absorbs and stores solar warmth from the sun to lessen the burden on the mechanical heating system.

Face-to-face meetings are common in the business world but slightly unexpected at home. However, in this craft-filled house, that's exactly what happens when owners—or visitors—walk into the pantry through this door, left.

The air-lock entry is imbued with a new sense of elegance in this house by architect George Buchanan, left. The door, which is punctuated by strips of glazing, is echoed by an identical inner door visible through the glass side panel.

Framed with exotic cherry and ash woods, this rustic-looking doorway connects one of two master bedrooms with a bath. Crossties fabricated from cherry wood stand out in front of a center panel of clear glazing.

Located in a Colorado vacation house designed by Aspen architect William Lipsey, the doors and bedroom illustrated on these two pages vividly show how historic themes can be restated in an exciting contemporary vein. For example, a doorway leading from one of two master bedrooms into a bath consists of elegant woods—cherry and ash—that have been finely sanded, finished, and enhanced with numerous coats of oil, left.

The darker cherry forms the frame and center crossties while the door is lighter ash. These materials, however, have been fabricated so that they resemble a rusticated version of Old West design with their simple, even spare, shapes and the crossbar at the very top extending beyond the vertical planks.

In the center, the crossties stand out visually in front of clear glazing, which frames a view of the elegant bath complete with a whirlpool tub. The glass is interrupted only by a small square of wood that contains the knob and other hardware.

The same motifs are interpreted differently in a door opening into the second master bedroom. Here, the idea of crossties is expanded with three bars stretching across the door, opposite left. The horizontal crossties, graduating in length as they descend, are made of an exotic cherry, while the entire door and frame is crafted in pale ash wood. These recall, says the architect, the days in the Old West when small window pieces of glass were held in place by wood mullions to create a large window. In this case, however, the backing is not glass but ash wood to ensure privacy in the bedroom.

The door opens into a bedroom that is highly detailed in a mixture of rough and clear materials. The most prominent element is a huge fixed skylight measuring 4 feet by 8 feet, opposite right. The skylight opens up the room and lends it the feeling of camping outside. The remaining part of the ceiling is clad with tongue-and-groove beadboard with an extra cut in the center so that it resembles the type of wainscoting found in many old stores and houses in the West.

The walls have been heavily textured by troweling a modern drywall compound to create a westernized striating effect. This impression of the historic is reinforced by a genuine old element—the structural pole. One of many strategically placed columns located throughout the house, it is made of spruce. Called standing deadwood, the pole is the remnant of a tree that died many years ago but never fell to the ground. Because some of the trees had survived forest fires before they died, they are heavily textured with scarring that is reminiscent of sculpture.

In this door, above, the cherry crossties are backed with solid ash wood to block the view from a hallway into the second master bedroom, right. Here, a large fixed skylight brightens the interior, which is a sophisticated blend of rustic materials.

This bathroom, left, bears the unmistakable influence of classicism. But it is also practical. The bathroom vanity, for example, contains a mirror and space to store toothbrushes and bathsoap. In another bathroom, however, grooming gear is stored in fine cabinetry made of cherry wood, opposite. The soaring mirror follows the angle of the sloped ceiling, making room for a round leaded-glass window embellished with the design of a unicorn.

Despite the recent emphasis on bathrooms filled with amenities such as whirlpool tubs and saunas as well as rich decorative effects, this room of the house, more than any other, remains utilitarian in its functioning and appearance. However, without making the bath look like a sybaritic retreat or an advertisement for a bath-fixture manufacturer, there are many inventive ways to make it a truly delightful space.

Take, for example, these two bathrooms designed by architect William Lipsey of Aspen, Colorado. In one, the man of the house gets to enjoy a bit of whimsy—and view a lovely piece of architectural detailing—every morning when he looks into the mirror to brush his teeth, wash his face, or shave.

The object of this delight is a "house" made of cherry wood that doubles as the bathroom vanity, above. Classically inspired, the vanity has a pedimented top embellished with dowels. It is supported—if not physically, at least symbolically—by two "columns," which are

actually interesting fluorescent lighting fixtures.

To complete this inviting bath, Lipsey specified a pedestal sink, a whirlpool tub, a rough-textured ceiling, and a visually striking glass-block wall.

The owner's daughter, on the other hand, has a bathroom that expresses her personal interests—primarily horses. Indeed, set right into the large mirror is a leaded-glass window decorated with the image of a unicorn. And, in keeping with the young lady's interest, the window looks out toward the horse barn. The horse motif repeats in the carpeting.

Like the rest of this vacation house, the bathroom represents an exciting blend of rough textures and fine woodwork. While the wall is clad with that common outdoor material—cedar shingles—the cabinetry is made of cherry wood and finished as it if were furniture, not storage space. The vanity is topped with DuPont Corian, which is also used as small squares in the cabinet doors, decorated with geometric patterns.

The beautiful wood columns designed by craftsman Mark McDonnell, shown here, not only frame the doorway of a splendid old house in Providence, Rhode Island, but they also shed light on the subject. For these columns are actually light fixtures that are made of a rock maple base and a poplar shaft painted with nautical blue acrylic enamel to simulate the smooth look of glass. At both the top and the bottom, the columns are burnished with a layer of contrasting 24-carat gold leaf.

Though the column format they assume is traditional, its application as a lighting fixture is most untraditional. "A traditional lamp has a base, a lampshade, and some sort of screw that holds the shade to the base," says McDonnell. "With our woodworking projects, I'm trying to make lamps that are unibody."

Stretching 78 inches high, the columns sit on a square base measuring 11 inches on each side. The columns taper as they rise from 7½ inches in diameter at the bottom to 6 inches at the top. The delicate tapering requires a great deal of handcraftsmanship, which McDonnell estimates took 50 hours of sanding for the pair. "And that's just the sanding, not the lathing," he adds.

Inside the top of each column, a spun-metal dish shields the wood from the heat generated by a 250-watt quartz halogen light. The lamp directs light up to the ceiling, which then reflects it down the walls. Because the fixtures are placed in the opening between a double living room, they were especially painted with the enamel acrylic for durability. Usually reserved for automobiles, this paint is extremely hardy. "It's very tough and can take a lot of abuse," says McDonnell. "And it won't fade for fifty years." To protect the gold leaf, a coat of clear lacquer has been applied. As a result, it can be cleaned with what McDonnell characterizes as "industrial-strength anything."

For practicality, the wiring for the lamps extends down through the center of the columns into the floor. A panel of switches in the living area controls the intensity of the light, which is governed by rheostats. A talented and versatile craftsman, McDonnell also works in glass.

Light columns by Mark McDonnell, each of which generates 250 watts of light, decorate a doorway between a double living room in a historic Rhode Island house. The column treatment is an eclectic blend of automotive paint and gold leaf.

The classical column has been rendered in a Westernized version in a house by William Lipsey with a rough marble base, a shaft of standing dead wood, and a capital of welded diamond-plate steel, above.

Soaring upward from the first floor of an open-plan house designed by architect Harry Teague, a structural column is mirrored by a less classical element—the flue of a woodburning stove, above, forming a balanced pair.

A column stands right in the center of a free-form boot-removal bench in a house by architect William Lipsey. The column is a weathered spruce tree trunk, the bench exotic cherry wood with oval edges reminiscent of a surfboard.

The column never seems to lose its appeal. A staple of classical architecture, it has been appropriated by every classical revival, Post-Modernism, and even by today's tract-house builders. The column has been rendered in a staggering variety of forms, from the Ionic to the Corinthian and Tuscan.

All columns can be broken down into two basic components: the column and the entablature. The column is composed of the base, the shaft, and the capital; the entablature is made up of the architrave, the frieze, and the cornice.

Today, thanks in large part to the availability of prefabricated columns, this architectural staple is enjoying an amazing renaissance. It comes as no surprise that craftspeople and craft-oriented architects are devising their own interpretations.

In the entry foyer of a house in Aspen, Colorado, architect William Lipsey gave the column he designed a Western flavor, left. The base is a piece of rough white marble from a regional quarry. The shaft is composed of a pole of standing deadwood, while the capital is a welded series of shapes fabricated from diamond-plate steel. "We sort of made our own Western order," Lipsey explains. The columns offer structural support for the foyer, which collects and stores solar heat in the stone floor and rear wall.

Harry Teague took an old tree trunk and converted it into a column and space divider in an open-plan house. When viewed from the bottom up, above left, the column appears to be placed in front of a mirror. In truth, the "reflected" image is the flue of a woodburning stove. The two form that most classical of design approaches—a balanced pair.

William Lipsey incorporated yet another of his Westernized columns in the main entry of a vacation house, above right. Here, the weathered spruce tree-trunk column is ringed by a boot-removal bench with oval edges. To offset the rustic appeal of the column, the bench is free form in its design and made out of cherry wood.

The bench was made with dovetailed joints that were cut, then glued together around the column so that the two elements do not touch.

The best way to conquer a siting problem, take advantage of the outdoor view, and expand usable living space in warm weather is to build a deck. That's what architect Christopher Woerner did for this house located on one of the Thimble Islands off the coast of Connecticut.

The beauty of this type of outdoor detail is that, because of the material used, the deck blends with rather than overwhelms the site. In fact, the deck enhances the site's usefulness by easing access to the water.

Embedded into solid rock, the deck cascades from the house via a series of levels. From the uppermost level, a wide set of steps frames the view of Long Island Sound. Their curve gently leads the visitor down toward the water, right. At the mid-level the deck flattens out to become a pleasant and sunny seating area. It functions beautifully as a secondary living area in warm weather, below. From there, a short flight of steps in a sharply defined triangular pattern connects the deck with the yard, which has been left in its natural state, opposite.

Artfully designed steps fanning out from a deck by architect Christopher Woerner frame a lovely view of—and lead down to—Long Island Sound from a house set on the storied Thimble Islands off the coast of Connecticut, above.

The multi-level deck terminates with three triangular steps that open into the yard area, opposite.

A seating area in the middle of the deck supplies extra space for entertaining and doubles as an outdoor living area in summer, left.

The Technique of
WOOD WORK

Noted for the exquisite cabinetry they fabricate, the craftspeople at Breakfast Woodworks in Branford, Connecticut, take great care during each step of the process. A woodworker carefully routs a slot that will join two planks in place, above.

With the channel clear, a layer of glue is applied by the woodworker inside each slot, above right. On the opposite edge of each board, a series of "pins" called splines are carefully hammered into the wood, left.

When the boards are joined, they are clamped together to dry to a perfect and practically seamless fit, left.

CHAPTER THREE

DETAILING WITH GLASS

Leaded-glass artistry by Ed McIlvane enlivens what would otherwise be a mundane three-panel space suitable only for tall, narrow casement windows. Beautiful glass is often used as a creative means for making a window into a room's focal point.

Birds take flight in a skylight designed in the foyer of a contemporary house, above. The ground consists of clear glass broken up by large squares of colored glass arranged in an asymmetrical fashion.

Glass is one of the most universal and versatile building tools architects and designers have available. Because it is transparent, glass promotes the flow of natural outdoor light into interior space, while its solid nature prevents the penetration of wind, rain, and snow. Indeed, the contradictory properties of glass once caused it to be characterized as a supercooled liquid, not a solid. That definition has been jettisoned in the twentieth century, and glass is now described as an inorganic product created by fusion. Almost all glass is composed of the same raw materials, including sand, soda, potash, lime, arsenic, and manganese. These are melted together in a hot furnace and then cooled to become glass.

Examples of primitive but beautiful glasswork have been discovered in ancient Egyptian ruins. The Romans, who made glass objects in molds, were the biggest producers of glass products in history until the process was mechanized in the nineteenth century. The art of glass blowing is believed to have been developed by the Syrians in the first century A.D. In Tudor England, many small, diamond-shaped pieces of hand-blown glass were combined to form large windows.

The loveliest examples of the craft, however, are what is commonly called stained glass and etched glass. In actuality, stained glass is a misnomer for two reasons. First, the pieces of glass are not stained, but either clear or permeated with color derived from various additives. Second, the glass is usually held in place, such as in a window, by strips of lead or, less commonly, copper foil. Thus, the proper term is "leaded glass."

There are many types of leaded glass, the loveliest example being the hand-blown variety, which is painstakingly created using a blowing pipe and a hot fire. Hand-blown glass is called "antique," although it can be old or new. This type of glass can be identified by the large number of air bubbles it has. Semiantique glass has fewer bubbles, while glass that is called "drawn antique" is machine made to resemble the hand-blown variety. Leaded-glass craftspeople also use a number of other types of glass. Some of these include "fractured streaky," "water glass," and "opalescent glass." Each is eminently suitable for different and specific purposes.

Etched glass, on the other hand, is simple plate glass that has been chemically treated. Generally in this chemical process, an abrasive eats away the top layer of glass, thus creating a frosted effect. Etched glass can best be described as the type used as door glazing in commercial office buildings in the 1950s. That utilitarian characterization, however, hardly does etched glass justice in an aesthetic sense. Indeed, etched glass lends itself to a wide range of visually appealing applications in both older and contemporary house styles.

Etched glass is probably most familiar for its use in old transoms. However, limiting etched glass to that one, and in most houses, outdated, application would be a mistake. Etched glass also makes for interesting kitchen cabinet doors, shower doors, tabletops, and light boxes, as well as decorative bandings to place around mirrors and picture frames.

Leaded glass readily lends itself to a wide range of architectural details. For example, clear leaded glass set in a window opening frames the outdoor view, while the rippling effect created by the air bubbles distorts the view and preserves indoor privacy. Colored leaded glass obscures an unsightly view, toward a garage, for example, and ensures indoor privacy all year long. A truly well-crafted detail combines both: a color design on a clear ground that makes the design seem to float in midair. But leaded glass has far more extensive applications for detailing than in windows.

One of the more unusual applications of leaded glass is in this skylight, opposite. Designed by architect Ric Weinschenk, this leaded-glass skylight illuminates the entryway of a contemporary house. While most of the skylight is composed of clear glass, it is punctuated by a fluid, abstract design in colored leaded glass. To contrast with the clear ground, the leaded glass is in shades of dark blue and violet. These sections are held in place by thick lead lines forming a grid that offsets the overall circular shape. To protect the skylight from the trajectories of errant baseballs, it is protected by a round frame that stretches up several feet and is incorporated into the exterior architectural styling.

In an older house, craftsman Ed McIlvane enlivened a bedroom with a three-part leaded-glass window that is placed in an existing opening. It is a beautiful detail that admits softly filtered light while preserving privacy, above. This project is a model for updating an existing house. When viewed up close, right, the blending of intricate shapes and colors becomes readily apparent. At the top, a rondel forms the focal point of each pane. It is visually supported by a strict geometry of squares in a range of blues, pinks, and grays.

The signature style of many a tract house—the shallow bedroom window— is renewed by the addition of leaded-glass panels, above. A rondel anchors the design, made up of a series of rectangles, below.

Tucked high on a wall in this striking contemporary house is a leaded-glass window that, though undeniably modern, embodies more than a little history. In fact, it is the family tree of the owners that craftsman David Wilson of South New Berlin, New York, rendered in an abstract fashion, opposite.

The 5-foot-square panel, which is set on one of its four points, echoes the interior detailing established by wood beams overhead and enhances the upper portion of the living room. However, while high glazing is generally specified to transmit and control interior light levels, this panel is an exception. It is purely decorative and effectively serves as a striking focal point.

The basic design is a simple geometric arrangement. The background consists of three stylized antique glass chevrons, inverted V shapes reminiscent of badges worn by sergeants in the U.S. Army. The smallest chevron is made of clear antique glass and is located at the bottom of the window. It interlocks with a slightly larger chevron of pale blue glass. Brilliant dark blue glass at the top of the window and alternating blue and clear glazing on the sides outline the largest chevron.

Superimposed on the background is the "tree" itself. The square core sits atop two rootlike extensions that represent the parents. One of them is in the national colors of Italy, orange, green, and white, symbolizing the husband. The other honors the mother and is in France's colors—red, blue, and white.

At the top are eight "branches," one for each of the children in the family. Boys are represented by blue; girls, red. The branches are supplemented by strips of clear and white remy glass, a type of leaded glass that is fabricated to be heavily textured, with swirling lines that distort the field of vision. Looking through it evokes the sense of peering through several feet of clear water to the bed of a lake or bay. The glass strips are separated and held securely in place by lead lines

Placed high on the wall of a contemporary house, far right, a 5-foot-square window by artisan David Wilson serves as an abstract family tree in the medium of leaded glass. Right, eight "branches" at the top represent the family's children.

When Wilson first became involved in the project, the owners emphasized their desire for a family tree. Though their thinking gravitated toward a literal representation, they gave the craftsman free rein to interpret their needs in his own way. While other artisans might have adapted a traditional design concept, a tree of life, for example, Wilson opted to work in the architectural mode that is part of his professional signature style. "My work is very flexible," he says. "I do totally different things for different clients. But at the same time, they look like they came from the same person." Other examples of Wilson's leaded-glass artistry are illustrated on pages 78 and 79.

The predominant shape in a remodeled kitchen—the sleek curve of the cooking peninsula—is echoed at the top of a leaded-glass window by A. J. Garber, left. While blocking a view of the garage, the window permits soft natural light to filter into the work area. Smoky gray and white glasses form a backdrop for brilliant stripes of transparent burgundy glass set in vivid diagonal patterns.

When the owners of this older house renovated their outdated kitchen, they called on artist A. J. Garber to design and fabricate a new, leaded-glass window to fit into an existing opening, above.

The result is an intriguing example of architectural detailing that succeeds on more than one level. In practical terms, the leaded glass obscures an unsightly direct view of the garage. On a purely aesthetic level, the curved lead lines in the glazing echo the shape of a work peninsula that juts into the room. "I almost always pick up on something like that," Garber says in explaining his approach to design decisions. "I select a strong architectural element in the space where the window will be located and build on that. This way, I develop a relationship between the window and the space instead of simply placing something in an opening where it is totally alien to what surrounds it."

At the same time, the window is set in opposition to the overall form of the house. Dating from the 1920s, the interior of the house is divided into well-defined rooms reserved for entertaining, cooking, dining, and so forth. To contrast with this orderly interior organization, Garber designed this window to incorporate an abundance of angles and curves.

The lead lines in many windows serve the strictly utilitarian function of holding the glazing in place. However, here they are integral to the design. In fact, Garber says, the lead lines "sometimes play a more important role than the colors because they define the shapes." In this window, the lead lines vary in width, with the curved portion being the thickest for added emphasis. "Because it has no color, the lead line had to be very strong visually to stand out," says Garber.

Contrasting with the curvilinear lead lines are stark diagonal lines that frame transparent, burgundy-colored, antique glass, which complements the overall color scheme of the kitchen. Other glass sections are in various tones of gray. Some of these are fairly transparent, which fills the kitchen with the outdoor light. Others are somewhat opaque, consisting of gray glazing that has been coated with a thin layer of white glass in a process called "flashing." The entire window is shielded from the debilitating effects of the weather by a large section of plate glass on the exterior.

Another striking window in a contemporary house designed by architect I. M. Pei is actually an architectural detail that tells a story. Designed by leaded-glass craftsman Ray King, this tall, narrow window fairly bubbles with exciting imagery.

Measuring a towering 12 feet high by a slim 27 inches wide, this detail replaced an existing window consisting of plain plate glass. It is set between two levels of the house where it masks from view an unattractive parking area behind, while illuminating both the stairwell and the living area below.

The most important element is at the top right, where two interlocking bands of gold represent the fiftieth wedding anniversary of the owners. Besides the wedding-band motif, the window includes "flying" pieces of tissuelike, pink flashed glass that has been sandblasted. The window also incorporates a "ribbon" of white glass that cascades from the top to the bottom. Throughout the piece are a riot of geometric objects such as cubes, cylinders, rectangular bars, and prisms. To break up the expanse of window visually, King created a grid of 1-inch thick leaded-glass strips that are separated by extremely thick lead lines measuring 1/16 inch. To avoid a static look, many of the decorative objects extend across these lead lines.

Though the window appears to be one tall expanse, it actually consists of two sections separated by a mullion. However, this is virtually impossible to see because of the colors of the glass and the bright outdoor light. In addition, many of the graphic elements are placed so that they span, or hop, the mullion.

A potpourri of geometric forms in this tall, narrow leaded-glass window by Ray King shed new light in the stairwell and living area of a contemporary house, left. Tucked at the top of the window are bands of gold-colored glass marking the owners' fiftieth wedding anniversary.

Opposite: An eyebrow window sheds new light on two levels in a renovated house. Besides illuminating the upper portion of the room, the leaded-glass window forms a strong focal point that emphasizes the height of the room.

When the owners of a traditional house undertook a thorough renovation, they opted for architectural contrast. One of the results was this airy, contemporary space at the rear of the house that soars two levels high to a lofty peaked ceiling.

The room is illuminated by large, fixed-pane windows placed so that they ''climb'' the open stairway. The arrangement is crowned by a modern rendering of a historic architectural element, the eyebrow window, opposite. Measuring 7 feet wide and 1 foot high at its tallest point, it is set beneath the peak of a sloped ceiling. Here, the window brings a view of trees and sky into both levels of the interior. In addition, it brightens and draws attention to the upper portion of the large-volume space.

When built, the opening was filled with ordinary plate glass. However, the owners, the Phillip Handler family, being adventurous in their design spirit, thought that this dramatic architectural detail deserved added emphasis. So they commissioned leaded-glass artist David Wilson to design a new window of leaded glass. It was fabricated by workers at the Cummings Studio in North Adams, Massachusetts.

Though Wilson was faced with the limitations of working within the existing opening, the owners gave him the freedom to design the new window however he thought best. ''It didn't have to satisfy any particular kind of aesthetic program in terms of a story the owners wanted to tell or any other sort of representational content,'' says Wilson.

That sort of design leeway enabled the artisan to render the age-old materials in a thoroughly modern manner. To ensure that the new window and the addition would be visually and aesthetically compatible, Wilson selected different glasses that echo the existing color scheme of the addition, white and lavender, subtly spiced with gray and clear glazing.

A delicate balance of subtly colored vertical and horizontal elements both emphasizes and ''contradicts'' the strong lateral plane of the actual window opening. For example, five lead lines that help hold the glass in place rise through the window, drawing the eye upward. These are echoed by a series of shorter lead lines in the center of the window, below. Giving these vertical elements added visual emphasis is the selection of clear glass that opens the upper room to a direct view of the treetops outside.

To reinforce attention to the horizontal shape of the window, Wilson broke up the shorter lead lines with a curving one. Besides adding to the sense of detailing in the design, it adds a sense of structural strength to the entire window. The clear glass is framed by two contrasting strips of ''colored'' glass that arc across the upper border of the window and extend down like columns, to become part of the base. The outer layer is opaque white; the inner one is a smoky gray. The simplicity of colors in the main body of the window is offset by an intricate foundation consisting of strips of gray placed above the light lavender. In the center, these strong lines are broken up by alternating rectangles of clear glass.

In selecting his materials and colors, Wilson was guided by the principle of contrast that he established with the basic design. For the clear portion, the artist specified remy glass, the heavily textured glass with swirly lines. The gray and lavender glass is transparent lead glass imported from West Germany.

In complete juxtaposition to this is the white, opaque ''flashed'' glass, which is composed of a thin layer of white glass that has been placed over and fused with a base layer. The base can be any color, but in this case it is clear. Commonly called ''fixture'' glass, flashed glass is the type of glazing made into lampshades, which are readily available on the mass market through department and lighting stores.

The eyebrow window is endowed with an added fillip of prominence by what was not done; hence, the fixed, rectangular windows below the eyebrow were left plain. With this approach, the rectangular windows form a visual base for the eyebrow without competing with it for the viewer's attention. Because the translucency of the glass is mostly retained in this project, the light from outside is allowed to flow into the room. In addition, one can see out to the view beyond. Other examples of leaded-glass work that craftsman David Wilson has done are illustrated on pages 74, 75, and 88.

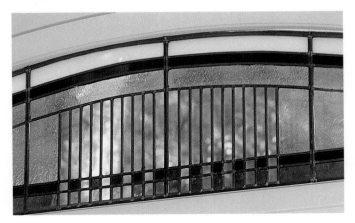

Above: The horizontal shape of the window is echoed by strips of opaque and transparent glass juxtaposed with subtle vertical lead lines. These are set upon a base that varies in color.

Windows take many shapes, but one of the most appealing is the crescent. Here are two very different examples of this historic form. Instead of mimicking history, however, the craftspeople imbued this traditional form with a contemporary sensibility.

In a new house designed by architect Ric Weinschenk, a crescent-shaped opening separates the breakfast nook and a hallway, below left. It gives the owners a view between the two spaces and encourages the flow of light for even levels of illumination.

The opening that Weinschenk specified is somewhat reminiscent of the fanlight window incorporated above the entry in many older styles of architecture. In this case, however, it has been greatly overscaled. In fact, it measures some 8 feet wide and 4 feet high in the center.

The crescent form readily lends itself to a modern interpretation of a Victorian lady's fan. For the fan portion, artisan Cynthia Legere selected clear, antique leaded glass, which is fabricated with a slightly swirling grain. The inner portion, or "handle," of the fan is made of blue water glass. During the manufacturing process, water glass is cooled so that actual ripples emerge. For structural support, Legere substituted brass rods for

some of the lead lines that form the struts of the fan. They are soldered over with copper foil in the manner of Louis Comfort Tiffany and concealed from view.

This piece is representative of Legere's work. She depends more on design and various textures of glass to create visual impact than on color. "A lot of my work has very little color so that it's not so overwhelming in a room," she says. "I don't want my windows to come out at people. I like subtle windows that depend more on design than color. In that way, they fit into the architecture rather than detract from it."

Equally subtle is a window by Ed McIlvane, below right. Though the shape befits the surroundings of a cathedral, this window is actually in a bathroom where it brightens the interior and enhances the sense of elegant detailing by mirroring other elements in the room. Simple and understated, the window is composed of ten sections of glass that are opaque to preserve privacy. The only colors—quiet pinks, grays, and blues—are placed in the border. Parallel lead lines throughout the piece visually emphasize the sectioning of the large opaque portion.

When the owners of an older house remodeled their

A. J. Garber's window in a remodeled dining room assumes the air of an abstract painting, below. In reality, it marks the spot where two awkward, shallow casement windows once framed a view of the house next door.

dining room, above, they asked A. J. Garber to contribute one of his abstract leaded-glass designs to the project. Out came two existing shallow casement windows of the type found in many tract houses of the 1950s and 1960s. In their place, Garber installed this fixed leaded-glass window that is a deft blend of hard geometric forms and highly contrasting colors. It measures approximately 6 feet by 3 feet. Unlike the original windows, which looked incomplete in their shallowness, the new one is imbued with a strong sense of presence. During the day, it reflects colors throughout the room. At night, it re-

sembles an abstract painting hung on the wall. And all year long, it blocks the view of the neighboring house that is quite close by.

The design alludes to the former window in several subtle ways. First, the gray and white sections at the top recall the panes of the original window. The line separating the grays and whites from the strong aqua at the bottom delineates the original window sashes. The upper portion of the window is composed of gray and white flashed glass. The lower portion, which consists of vibrant yellow, red, and aqua, is almost totally opaque.

Karl Raseman solved a common problem facing owners of older houses. When he added a sun room along the rear wall of his forty-year-old house, a window to the outdoors suddenly became a window to the indoors. While the need for daylighting remained, the issue was complicated by the need for privacy and the desire to still maintain a view through the "transparent" glass-encased addition.

Raseman, a glass artisan who lives on Long Island, New York, deftly solved the problem by designing and fabricating this fanciful window. Besides enabling outdoor light to penetrate through the sunroom into his living room, it ensures privacy and insulates the interior against the winter cold.

But the window has other advantages. It adds a dash of color to an otherwise monochromatic room and functions as the focal point of the living area. In addition, the window can easily be taken out, thus becoming a sort of movable portfolio of Raseman's work. The artist and his partner, Vincent Winsch, operate Creative Glass Works in Setauket, Long Island.

Because the window no longer opens to the outdoors, it was fabricated as a nonoperable window that is fixed in place. Unlike other examples of glass craftsmanship illustrated in this chapter, this project has a clear ground composed of ordinary window glazing. "It's the same type of glass you would find in a typical window in any house," he says. The result is a ground that, though transparent, adds to the visual impact of the window by fostering the illusion that the center design is floating on its own in space.

The design, a vertical open-sided box, seems to turn inside as the eye of the viewer moves from top to bottom. The effect is reminiscent of *trompe l'oeil* painting, although usually *trompe l'oeil* is thought of in terms of paint that imitates the look of marble, wood, or other more elaborate surface finishes.

This particular inverted perspective is inspired by the work of M. C. Escher, a Dutch graphic artist whose work was much seen in the 1950s and 1960s. "The majority of his work did not make sense in terms of true perspective," Raseman explains. "As you look at this panel, you realize that the box really makes no sense at all. It could never be manufactured. It can only be done on a flat surface."

Much of Raseman's glass detailing is based on Escher's ideas, and the Long Island artist has spent much of his time trying to translate the Dutch artist's graphic work into the medium of glass. Many of Raseman's materials, on the other hand, are inspired by the work of Louis Comfort Tiffany.

While the ground is clear window glazing, the black, gray, and white portions of the design are made of different varieties of opalescent glass. The lines of the design are broken up by several "balls," which are composed of a type of glass called "fractured streaky." This particular glass was usually used by Tiffany as a background for floral designs in his famous leaded-glass windows at the turn of the century. It incorporates tiny flakes of colored glass upon which is fused a solid sheet of glazing during fabrication. "If you run your hand over the back of the ball," says Raseman, "you can feel many tiny chips of glass."

Fractured streaky is manufactured in a number of color combinations. These particular ones are transparent glass with bits of purple, red, and pink flakes. For even more color, Raseman added strips of purple cathedral glass, aqua Flemish glass, and dark blue water glass. The latter have large air bubbles that distort the view. The numerous pieces of glass are held in place using another technique that dates back to the early twentieth century: copper foil. This method was also used by Tiffany and is most readily seen in his lampshades. It allows the craftsperson to work easily with smaller pieces of glass than would ordinarily be practical with lead.

In designing this fascinating window panel, Raseman worked with a full-scale drawing of the opening it would fit into, which measures 5 feet by 2½ feet.

Window on the World: A geometric design based on the work of graphic artist M. C. Escher seems to float in space in the living room of leaded-glass craftsman Karl Raseman. The effect results from combining clear window glazing with a variety of leaded glasses.

To maximize the amount of daylight allowed indoors, contemporary architects have harkened back to the lunette, a fixed pane of glazing above a window. An old tradition, this technique is as suitable today as it was in the nineteenth century. Yet it presents architects, interior designers, and homeowners with the problem of selecting an appropriate window treatment that encourages the flow of light to the indoors yet preserves privacy.

The dilemma was solved by four craftspeople who filled the lunette openings with leaded-glass designs that add an exquisite sense of interior detailing without compromising their original purpose.

Al Garber, an experienced lead-glass artist, deftly integrated art and modern architecture with the arches he designed for a condominium unit, below. Faced with an existing opening, which was originally designed by the developer and echoes actual arches throughout the building, Garber conceived a design that becomes the focal point of the room and adds an artful crown to the ordinary sliding glass patio doors beneath.

The base of the design is a series of horizontal lines of glass that draw the eye laterally across the window. They are neatly separated by an archlike piece of two-way mirror. During the day, it affords a view outdoors; at night, it reflects light back into the room.

The need for sufficient light levels while maintaining privacy asserts itself most vividly in bathroom design. Philadelphia craftsman Joe Beyer solved the dilemma with a lovely stained glass window and lunette that pre-

serves the view to the backyard in a contemporary master bath, opposite above left.

The family has several children, and "the house is always brimming with activity," says Beyer. The owners wanted a very private and quiet adult getaway for themselves. Beyer reinforced the theme of the room by dispensing with drapery and other traditional window treatments in favor of leaded glass.

A black whirlpool tub and white walls gave the artist a clean canvas, so he chose pale, restful colors: pink, green, blue, and purple, all tinged with gray. Supplementing this palette is clear, textured glass called "seedy flint," which has many tiny air bubbles. The design is a highly stylized interpretation of the foliage found on a gingko tree, set beneath the view of a purple moon.

Translucent glass has been fashioned into a striking design by Maya Radoczy of Seattle, Washington, in a remodeled New York City brownstone, opposite above right. The design encompasses three fixed lunettes above a bay window, providing color for the white walls and uniting the three 2½-foot-tall sections of glass.

While the design is abstract, it is not architectural. Instead, the organic design seems to flow from pane to pane despite the interruption created by the 9-inch mullions. Included in the design are circles, known as "rondels," that were hand blown by the artisan. The translucent glass Radoczy chose is also hand-blown antique glazing imported from Europe.

An entirely different approach was taken by Janet Redfield of Harborside, Maine, when she designed and fabricated a leaded-glass window for a new house, opposite below. Set directly over a desk in an at-home office area, the fixed lunette is alive with the excitement of a flock of birds in flight.

The design is arranged so that when viewed from below, the glass birds seem to fly through, or perch on, the branches of a real tree outdoors. To enhance the feeling of realism, the wings of the birds are three-dimensional, protruding from the lunette by 3 and 4 inches. They were cut by hand and attached by the artist before installation.

The designs of the birds are an amalgamation of realism and fantasy. A fairly literal representation of a bluebird is juxtaposed next to an imaginative bird that can be seen only on this window—and in the mind.

Because the lunette is directly above a large fixed window that brightens the room, Redfield opted for a clear ground. By not using a dark ground, she avoided creating excessive amounts of contrast that would have prevented the viewer's eye from adjusting between the light and dark glazing and would have unnecessarily reduced the light level in the work space.

Al Garber transformed a potential design liability, an existing arch added above sliding glass doors, into the focal point of a living room by designing this lovely lunette.

A three-part lunette by Maya Radoczy crowns a bay window in a dining nook of a remodeled brownstone. The abstract, yet fluid, design flows across 9-inch mullions creating a sweep of color and design.

A leaded-glass lunette and window design by Joe Beyer pours light into a master bath while preserving both the outdoor view from a whirlpool tub and privacy. The design, which is adapted from the gingko tree, rises through operable casement windows into the fixed-glass lunette.

A flock of birds is caught forever soaring into flights of fantasy in a leaded-glass lunette by Janet Redfield. Adding to the realistic effect is her imaginative touch of fabricating the wings so that they protrude outward from the glass.

One of the significant developments in post-1960s housing has been the renovation of older houses by young buyers. Part of this trend is a reaction to the financial hardship involved with buying a new house. Eager to live in established neighborhoods that, in most cases, are close to the city's center, these new owners adopted the old houses and adapted them to meet the needs of the 1980s.

One of the details these new owners encounter is the transom, a glass opening above doorways. Usually, the transom consisted of a wood frame fitted with a single pane of frosted glass. On hot days, the frame could be opened for flow-through ventilation without leaving the door ajar. Whether the transom was open or shut, light flowing through the glass panel brightened the hallway within.

The transom is rarely incorporated into architecture built today. It was eliminated by the advent of central air conditioning, which did away with the need for interior ventilation pathways, and open planning. That in turn reduced the number of hallways and interior doorways in houses built after World War II.

Yet the transom has not lost any of its practicality in older houses, particularly if the existing wiring dictates the use of window air-conditioning units and remodeling leaves the center hallway intact. Hence, the transom has been put to good, though unorthodox, use in a few new houses. One, for example, is this house in Connecticut. Though the architecture by Peter Jackson is contemporary in every respect, the house includes a transom.

The reasons are simple and practical. The owners wanted to exploit daylight that pours into an at-home office to illuminate a center stairwell. Atop the interior door connecting the stairwell and the office, Jackson and the owners designed an overscaled transom measuring 3½ feet wide and 2½ feet high. Because air flow was not a consideration, the transom was not designed to be operable. And though the owners wanted the light from the outdoors, they did not want the view, which they found to be disrupting as they walked up and down the stairs during the day.

To ensure the flow of light while obscuring the view,

owners and architect called on Sandy Moore of Guilford, Connecticut. Moore, an etched-glass artisan with the "heart of an illustrator," as she puts it, designed a transom that exactly fills the bill. Emblazoned with the design of a snail, the plate-glass transom soaring over the door adds a welcome bit of detailing both in the all-white stairwell and in the adjoining office. At the same time, it beautifully fulfills its design mission.

To leave the design free of unnecessary visual clutter, any small details have been eliminated, resulting in a streamlined, though realistic, picture of the snail. Because the owners wanted the view blocked, Moore etched the ground of the transom panel, as well as details within the snail design. The body of the snail was masked during the etching process and remains clear.

For design motifs to use in her work, Moore frequently turns to nature. The best source of designs, she insists, is books, including collections of wallpaper and fabric patterns. Since these designs are flat and two-dimensional, they are easily adaptable to glass.

Moore began her professional art career as a fashion illustrator. In that job, she was faced with the problem of creating an image in black and white without the aid of any other colors. She carried over the lessons she learned there to her glass etching. To compensate for the lack of color, Moore creates a simple but visually vivid shape, the shell, for example, on which the viewer's eye can focus. "It's not unlike black-and-white photography in that a fine newspaper photograph has an extremely strong image," she says. In addition, she usually places the design slightly off center to create a sense of friction that adds to the visual impact.

Besides use in transoms, etched glass has many other applications. It can be placed in windows to block an unsightly view or enhance privacy in rooms that face a busy street. Etched glass also makes for unique shower doors, translucent dividing screens, tabletops, light boxes, and decorative bandings for picture frames.

A step-by-step guide to how etched glass is made, with another example of Sandy Moore's work, is shown on pages 122 and 123. Other examples of her work appear on pages 92 and 93.

Above: Nestled atop a doorway, a generously oversized, contemporary transom filled with a pane of etched glass filters light into a stairwell.

Patterned after a chambered nautilus, this shell is clear plate glass with etched details and background.

Lead-glass artist David Wilson has worked on many church windows, so when he was offered a different sort of project, he jumped at the opportunity. The project was to design a door and transom for a house in Connecticut to fill an existing opening. Given a wide latitude of creativity by the owners, Wilson designed this striking doorway with unmistakable Art Deco overtones, left.

The doorway and transom, already an impressive 10 feet high, are heightened optically by the vertical design. It is enhanced with curves formed by "slicing" ovals in half and setting them toward each other in the door and against each other in the transom. They function as "a play on ovals" within the overall design, according to Wilson. Besides its unusual height, the doorway, which connects the living room and a patio, is also marked by an impressive blend of materials.

The design is an opulent mix of white opalescent, bluish gray opaline, and clear glass. Opaline glass is half transparent and half opaque. Completing this visual potpourri are two strips of mirror that streak upward through the center and along each side of the transom. In the doorway below, the silver color of the mirror is repeated in the paint on the frame.

The lead lines that hold this eclectic mix of colors and materials in place emphasize the vertical lines. Contrasting with these are a series of horizontal lead lines that draw the eye laterally across the transom. These lead lines are reinforced by ½-inch-thick reinforcing bars that serve as mullions and ensure structural support for the door as it is repeatedly opened and closed.

The visual effect of this Art Deco doorway is quite dramatic. The clear glass enables the viewer to see through the door to the area beyond. At the same time, the white, opaque glass sections function as visual barriers, while the mirroring reflects the interior of the room. "Several images are at work in the door," explains Wilson. "There is the surface of the door itself; the reflected images in the surface of the mirror; and the exterior images that you see through the clear glass. Because the eye is seeing all three planes at once, it gets extremely complex." Other examples of Wilson's work in leaded glass are shown on pages 74, 75, 78, and 79.

Art Deco splendor is readily evident in this leaded-glass door and transom designed by David Wilson. What might have been an uninspired connecting element between a living room and a patio becomes a riveting architectural detail that mixes clear and opaque glass with strips of mirror. The 10-foot height of the overall doorway is further heightened by a vertical design tempered by ½-inch-thick lateral steel-reinforcing bars placed in the door.

The front door of this house on an island off the Maine coast is also special. It neatly sums up the environment by incorporating universal and local motifs: a fish, the sea, an island, and a great blue heron. The custom design is by Janet Redfield, a Maine-based lead-glass artist.

The use of leaded glass in the door was actually the second choice by the owners and Redfield. But it proved to be a wise decision. Though the owners knew they wanted to add leaded-glass detailing to their new house, they originally thought the appropriate place would be at the very peak of the house in the form of a huge triangular window. But once Redfield and the owners discussed the project, they realized the site would not work. "Anybody wanting to look at the window would have had to roll their head all the way back and look straight up in the air 40 or 50 feet," recalls Redfield.

The solution? Relocate the leaded glass to a spot where it would be easier to see and enjoy. And what better spot than at the front door where it welcomes guests and filters soft light into the entry? From the indoors, the oval frames a view of a patio and woods.

Fabricated in the shape of an oval, the leaded-glass panel measures 3½ feet high and 14 inches wide. It is fitted into a standard panel door. Because privacy is not an issue, since the house is secluded at the end of a mile-long driveway, Redfield was free to choose a ground of clear hand-blown glass. This created a completely blank canvas for her design.

In the lower portion of the oval is a stylized fish, "a fantasy fish," Redfield describes it, beneath a blue water line in the center of the oval. Also in the middle is a large brown island and, at the top, a realistic interpretation of a great blue heron. Except for the heron's neck, which is made of white opalescent glass, the entire oval consists of blown, or antique, glass imported from Germany. The heron motif fits naturally into the design as it is the type of shore bird commonly found in a waterside environment. Though subtle, it and the other elements within the design give the entryway, as well as the house, a unique sense of place. In addition, it reflects Redfield's penchant for using naturalistic forms. Other examples of her work are shown on pages 82 and 83.

Welcoming guests to a secluded retreat on an island off the coast of Maine is this front door containing a leaded-glass oval, which serves as a microcosm of the seaside environment. Designed and made by Maine resident Janet Redfield, it blends the vibrant colors of a fish, water, islands, and a bird that stand out vividly on a clear ground. The oval is made almost entirely of hand-blown glass, giving it a sense of delicacy and winsome grace.

Doorways are often thought of merely as openings that facilitate movement into and out of a house or room. In the hands of inventive craftspeople, however, these utilitarian openings can assume a life of their own. The work of Kenneth von Roenn, for example, is replete with rich materials and intriguing design motifs. For a house in Connecticut undergoing extensive remodeling, he designed an entry that literally stops traffic on the street.

The entry consists of a doorway flanked by fixed panels. Above these run a shallow transom. Including the mullions between the door and the side panels, the entry is 7 feet wide. Hand-blown rondels that are 3 inches in diameter are inserted into squares of opaque brownish-gray glass that blocks the view from the outdoors and preserves the owners' privacy, right. Running across the entire face of the entry is a broken, 9-inch-deep stripe of red, translucent hand-blown antique glass. Throughout the design, von Roenn emphasizes contrast, one of his basic design themes. For example, round elements are juxtaposed with rectangles, which in turn are set against circles and squares.

Indoors, the house opens to the rear with a glass wall that spans across the back and around each side. This expanse of glass brings a view of Long Island Sound into the house. The red stripe in the entry is placed directly on the same line of the horizon as where the water meets the sky.

The interplay of elements in the entry takes place within a grid formed by ½-inch-square antique crystals. The antique glass obscures from view everything except vague forms and colors, therefore ensuring indoor privacy. The square grid is most vividly illustrated from the indoors, opposite above. Equally enticing from the indoor view are a series of lead support bars of varying thicknesses that radiate out from the door into the side panels and up into the transom. They have been incorporated into the design to strengthen the door, which must be opened and closed, and they visually unite it with the side panels and the transom. The bars are fabricated and installed so that they become fluid gestures that give the entry a sculptural relief that helps to break up the overall geometry.

While von Roenn's work is unabashedly abstract, a

Highly abstract forms have been combined by Kenneth von Roenn in designing and making this inviting entry in a remodeled house in Connecticut, above.

leaded-glass doorway and wall in a Rocky Mountain vacation house is highly realistic, below opposite. Designed by Garrett Hancock of Sylvan Garrett in Dallas, the 28-foot-long by 8-foot-high expanse was fabricated by Bruce W. Shelton. Set between the living room and the television room, the glass wall and door reflect the outdoor scenery: snow-laden mountains, clouds, and sky. The wall is completely different when viewed from each side. The center portion of the clouds is composed of clear glass so visitors in the TV room can look directly out through the living room to the seven hills of Aspen. On the living room side where this photograph was taken, the wall appears to mirror the outside view. The white ''clouds'' are blended with green ''mountains'' and a variety of blues for the sky. All the glass is held in place by copper-foil wrapping.

A large landscape made of glass reflects the environment surrounding a house in Aspen, right. The scenic door serves as a wall dividing the living room and the TV room.

Intriguing structural elements reveal themselves when the entry is viewed from the indoors, right. Easily visible is the grid formed by 1½-inch square antique glass crystals. Fluidly curved support bars fan out from the doorway into the side panels and up into the transom.

Translucent leaded glass preserves the free flow of space in a high-rise apartment while deftly separating the dining area from the kitchen, left, and the kitchen from the foyer, opposite left. Fabricated by Maya Radoczy, the doors are composed of clear glass with additional hints of color, primarily pinks and pale greens.

Large rondels form the center row of this striking doorway by Dale Chihuly. The side panels are clear, cast glass decorated with drawings by Flora Mace.

The interior doorway of many modern houses and apartments is often visually uninteresting. Yet in the hands of talented artisans, doorways can be transformed from humdrum to intriguing, as the examples shown on these pages illustrate. When a couple bought two apartments in the luxury Trump Plaza high-rise in New York City, they brought in architect Richard Lewis to undertake a thorough remodeling. Seeking to maintain a sense of openness, Lewis and the owners decided to use translucent doors between the dining area and the kitchen, as well as between the kitchen and the foyer.

Though they insisted on translucency, the clients did not want the commonly specified alternative, glass block. They called upon artisan Maya Radoczy to design and fabricate these lovely leaded-glass doors. Separating the dining area from the kitchen are two sets of pocket doors, above, which were decorated with rows of leaded glass set laterally to emphasize the width of the doorway. Structural support is incorporated into the design in the form of reinforcing bars. Some are set horizontally every few panels, while others run vertically at an angle.

Radoczy took the same approach in fabricating the doors and transom that separate the kitchen from the foyer, opposite left. Both designs establish a strong grid, particularly the doors in the foyer, which are topped by a 7-foot-wide transom. In this case, however, the lateral design is enhanced by a free-form interpretation of what the artist calls "microforms." As she explains, "These are vaguely organic in nature but not really definable."

The owners of this house can bask in the reflected glory created by small pieces of two-way mirror set in these French doors composed of clear, light brown, and gray leaded glass by Joe Beyer.

Both projects are composed of clear antique glass supplemented by small pieces of pink and green glass that is highly textured to allow the passage of light through the doors while blocking the view. Other examples of Radoczy's glass work are illustrated on pages 84 and 85.

In the Rhode Island home of Jacques and Lorraine Hopkins, legendary leaded-glass craftsman Dale Chihuly, in collaboration with Flora Mace, fabricated this striking door that connects the foyer with the living room, opposite below. Chihuly, who lives in Seattle, Washington, used large hand-blown rondels that were cut into rectangles and placed in the center openings. The rondels are emblazoned with vibrant colors that grow progressively fainter as the eye moves outward from the center. In addition, these panels were treated with a chemical "fuming" process, creating an irridescent appearance that is reminiscent of the glasswork created by Louis Comfort Tiffany.

The side panels are clear cast glass decorated with an-

imal and floral designs by Mace, who also lives in Seattle. While the glass enables light to flow from the living room into the foyer, the swirling effect of the rondels and the decoration on the side panels obscures the view, ensuring the Hopkins's privacy. For structural support, the mullions and the frame are made of metal and are set inside the wood door.

What could have been merely a mundane set of French doors separating a foyer and a living room was elevated to a high level of sophistication by artisan Joe Beyer, above right. At the client's request, the design is abstract and limited to a narrow color range of hand-blown clear, light brown, and gray glass spiced with small bits of two-way mirror glazing, somewhat similar to that used in high-rise International Style office buildings. Depending on which room is illuminated, the two-way mirroring either reflects light or enables the viewer to see through to the other space. As Beyer describes it, "As you walk by the door it kind of sparkles and winks at you a little."

Because it emphasizes spare, clean lines, modern architecture is often denigrated as cold, austere, even antihuman. The opposite, in fact, is true. The airy, open floor plans of modern houses encourage exploration of the interior landscape, while window walls and other devices draw attention to the outdoors and help unite structure and site. The modern house forms a perfect backdrop, like a blank canvas, upon which homeowners are free to express their interests without having to worry about an aesthetic clash between their decor and the architecture of the house.

Employing detailing in the modern house is often viewed as a thoughtful way to use quality, industrially inspired materials. There are other ways, however, to stamp the modern house with one's own personality. That was the approach taken by Charles and Beth Derby when they designed and built a contemporary house in Guilford, Connecticut. Their interest in Oriental art is evident in the decor of the house, which is spare, subtle, and monochromatic. Indeed, the neutral color scheme is punctuated by a solitary burst of color—the rich red of a robe that is prominently displayed as a wall hanging in the living room.

Today, craftspeople are enlivening etched glass with decorative designs to produce inventive detailing. Asked to contribute to this house, glass artisan Sandy Moore decorated a pair of glass French doors with etched designs that extend the owners' interest in Oriental art to the architectural shell itself, opposite left. Incorporated into a window wall, the glazed doors open the living room to a view of a sun-splashed atrium filled with plants. The etched-glass designs also reinforce the personal imprint of the owners on the architecture. The selection of the technique of etching preserves the view into the atrium, and allows light to flow into the living room. At the same time, the doors insulate the living area from winter drafts. In addition, the etched doors become a detail that can be seen and enjoyed from both the living room and the atrium.

The design of the etching is simple and imbued with the spirit of the Orient. On one glass panel is a crane standing on one leg. The other panel is decorated with tall stalks of bamboo. To unite the two panels, Moore etched a sea of water that visually "swims" from one panel to another.

With etched glass, there are two approaches. In the first, the artisan etches the design, leaving the background clear. In the second, this process is reversed. A design is drawn onto the glass and masked with tape so that it remains clear, and the background is etched. In this project, the decorative motifs are etched glass, and the background is clear glass. The step-by-step process of fabricating an architectural detail is shown with more of Sandy Moore's work on pages 100 and 101.

Moore gave prominence to the water and injected a note of realism by adding the visual effect of glue chipping. An old technique, glue chipping involves applying a form of animal glue to the etched glass. The glue is dried slowly by a complicated process, until it is almost set. Then the glass is placed in the sun so that the final drying occurs quickly. As the glue dries, it tightens and cracks, and then it begins to flake off, creating random crystal patterns on the glass, opposite right.

With this technique, Moore created a prismatic effect that scatters light and causes the glue-chipped glass to shimmer, much like real water does when it is struck by bright sunlight. The glue-chipped glass is broken up by small areas of clear glass designed to resemble stylized animals and plants.

Moore drew the designs on the glass freehand, based on artwork she found in books illustrating birds and those showing typical Japanese designs. She then adapted these designs to the door's dimensions. For this project, ¼-inch plate glass measuring 20¼ inches wide by 69¾ inches long was used. The panels are held in place by oak door frames, which were made by owner Charles Derby.

The contrast of the modern style house with the tradition of the Oriental style—as conveyed in the doors and other decorative elements in the house—is striking.

Above: Adding sparkle to the water is an effect called "glue chipping," which consists of drying an application of animal glue on a portion of the etched glass. Tiny "plant" forms have been left clear for contrast.

Left: Etched-glass doors mark a definite but discreet separation between the living area and an atrium in a contemporary house in Connecticut. The Japanese-inspired etched designs, a crane on one panel, bamboo on the other, are visually unified by a sea of sparkling water below.

Craftsman Mark McDonnell of Providence, Rhode Island, blended art and function in a house in New Haven, Connecticut, when he created a jewel of a wall sconce in a stylized diamond shape, below left.

The large background measures 54 inches long and 22 inches wide at its broadest point. On the sides, the background curves at a sharp angle, giving the sconce a three-dimensional appearance that makes the piece appear to hover on the wall when it is viewed from the side. The background is made of vitrolite, a type of highly reflective black glass that was manufactured in the 1930s and 1940s and incorporated into kitchens and bathrooms, as well as into the façades of pharmacy stores. The bowl is composed of a particularly lovely white opaque glass imported from Germany, on which tiger's eye stones have been carefully glued.

Vitrolite glass also forms the background for another sconce by McDonnell that is one of a pair crowning a multistory stairwell in a Bristol, Rhode Island, home, below right. In this case, however, the sconce assumes the shape of an arrowhead that towers 55 inches high to become a striking focal point for the stairway. At its widest point, the sconce measures 20 inches.

The sconces can be brightened and dimmed with a switch set in the adjacent wall. And though both have the geometric appearance associated with Art Deco design, McDonnell says he was inspired by his interest in German Expressionist architecture. The visual effect of the sconces is enhanced by their large sizes, so that they transcend the utilitarian category of light fixtures to become illuminated sculptures.

McDonnell created an entirely different light source for the library of the Smith home, opposite above. These lamps consist of opaque glass that was hand blown into a conical shape. They are decorated with swirls of dark blue glass on the exterior that resembles running water. This visual effect was achieved by applying drops of the blue glass onto the shade as it was being turned.

Measuring 19 inches high, the lamps stand on square bases made of poplar wood painted with dark blue nautical paint, generally reserved for the hulls of sailboats. Again, "showcase" bulbs are used. Unlike conventional round bulbs that create a bright pool of light at the bottom, leaving the top dark, the showcase bulbs throw off a shaft of illumination that is consistent from top to bottom.

Besides serving as a practical lighting source, the lamps are so tall they appear to be large vases when turned off. As a result, they are equally intriguing whether they are off or on. "A lot of lamps work visually only one way or the other," McDonnell says, explaining his design approach. "To me, it's important that they look good when they're not in use."

Details can become the focal point of a room when rendered in large-scale fashion, as Ray King did when he designed a unique chandelier that measures approximately 6½ feet across, opposite below. To fit beneath the 9-foot-high ceiling, the chandelier measures only 18 inches high.

This unusual piece has six sides, or facets. It is best observed by looking at the elements on one side of the chandelier from left to right. On the far left is a "fin" composed of white optical glass. It has been sandblasted, or etched, so that it glows. Next is a thin strip of turquoise glass and a large area of gray anodized aluminum. Small "puncture" openings filled with crystal lenses enable pinpoints of light to spill into the room. At the opposite end of the chandelier, a section of "ribbed" glass, much like that usually seen in a dentist's work light, glows softly. On the extreme right side is another section of red anodized aluminum.

Though unusual, the chandelier is an extremely practical light source. The bulb inside creates a shaft of light directly down the center of the fixture for low-level illumination. These bulbs are aimed upward so that their light "bounces" off the ceiling and helps to add a brightness to the entire room.

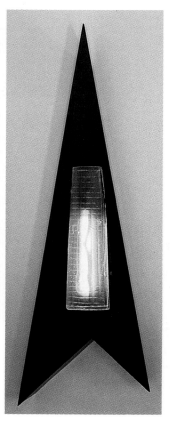

Beautiful wall sconces shed new light in the form of stylized diamonds, above, and an arrowhead, right. Both are based on the aesthetic of German Expressionist architecture.

A pair of mantel lamps attract the eye whether they are turned off or on, left. Their vaselike conical shape is composed of white opaque glass decorated with swirls of dark blue glass reminiscent of the sea. A striking chandelier illuminating a library contains both glass and metal, below. It is composed of six facets and measures an impressive 6-foot-4-inches long.

In this shady garden, guests are invited to sit on two highly unusual benches made from an unexpected material—glass. The benches, right, were designed and made by craftsman Howard Ben Tré of Providence, Rhode Island.

Designed for this particular garden, the motifs bear classical overtones inspired by an existing stone bench elsewhere in the garden. Based on classical Etruscan elements, but not literal interpretations of them, the benches, as Ben Tré describes it, "combine classical forms with a Moderne sensibility." For example, when viewed from the front, each bench has a strong silhouette shape. Yet each side section incorporates a columnlike form capped by a stylized entablature, far right.

The visual effect is quite stunning. While the benches appear thick and massive, that image is softened by the light look created by glass. The effect is reinforced by sunlight. On bright days, light penetrates but does not pass through the glass, thus making the benches glow. At other times, they appear to be a rich green, the same color found on the edge of a thick, plate glass tabletop.

The benches are made of solid glass cast much like bronze sculpture. Each bench consists of three pieces, a seating slab and two side supports, joined and supported structurally by a copper frame. First, Ben Tré made a form out of a flexible plastic similar to Styrofoam. Around the form, the craftsman packed a chemically treated sand compound that hardens after one or two hours. Using special tools, he dug out the plastic, leaving the sand mold, which weighs between 400 and 500 pounds.

Molten glass was ladled into the mold at a factory and placed in a cooling oven, which uses computer technology to gradually lower the temperature of the glass to normal levels. Six weeks later, the glass had hardened and the sand mold gradually disintegrated. Sandblasting removed any remaining sand residue, leaving the pieces ready to be polished.

Because attaching one piece of glass to another creates a weak point, each section of the bench is connected to a network of copper bars. These run beneath the seating slab and inside each side section. When someone sits on one of the benches, one's body weight is transferred from the glass to the metal and, in turn, to the stone patio. Each bench will support 300 pounds. The copper bars, which slide into each other, can be disassembled, allowing the benches to be taken apart and moved.

Placed in a shady area of the garden, the benches are exposed to only brief periods of direct sunlight, thus protecting them from potential cracking and other effects of weathering. Far from burdensome, routine maintenance is simple and, indeed, rather matter of fact: an occasional spraying with the garden hose.

Ordinary glass has been magically transformed by Howard Ben Tré into two unique benches that invite guests to linger and enjoy the views and fragrances offered by a shady garden. These objects of functional design solve the practical need for seating with an aesthetic wish for a strong horizontal design element. On bright days, the benches absorb sunlight and literally glow. At other times, their dominant color is green, which adds to the springlike atmosphere of this restful retreat.

The Technique of

ETCHING GLASS

1

Cover the entire pane of glass with a sheet of thin tracing paper that is secured in place with tape at each corner. Then draw the desired design to full scale.

2

Remove the tracing paper, clean the work surface with commercial glass cleaner, and cover it with one layer of masking tape. Overlap tape edges to create seams.

3

Place a sheet of carbon paper and then tracing paper over the taped glass, again securing the edges with adhesive tape. Retrace the design with a ballpoint pen.

4

Remove the tracing and carbon papers. Cut along the lines of the design, including interior details, with a sharp-tipped knife. For best results, change blades frequently.

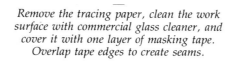

5

Peel tape off the area to be exposed to the abrasive effect of etching, either the design or the background. Leave the area that is to remain clear covered with protective tape.

THE ART of etching glass is surprisingly simple. The steps outlined on these pages for designing and preparing the glass are those followed by artisan Sandy Moore. The process, when used by other craftspeople, may vary.

In planning an etched-glass project, one must consider whether to use an etched background with a clear design or vice versa.

Moore generally chooses standard ⅛-inch-thick window glass for her work. Projects that must endure continual handling, however, such as the kitchen cabinet doors shown on the right, require thicker glass.

For doing the actual etching, Moore relies on a cemetery monument-making company. There, workers use high-pressure air-compression equipment to sandblast the glass with aluminum oxide or silicon carbide dust. This is the safest method. Other techniques call for hydrofluoric acid compounds in either liquid or paste. The liquid acid requires special equipment, air ventilation, and expertise often unavailable to the casual craftsperson. The paste form is sold by many art supply stores.

In a remodeled Victorian house, artisan Sandy Moore has enlivened ordinary kitchen cabinet doors with the subtle beauty of etched glass. In this application, the panels visually soften the expanses of white while reinforcing the geometric detailing. The glass panes are held in place in the doors by strips of decorative wood molding. The bulb in the onion design here has been left clear and the ground etched, blocking a view of the cabinets' contents. It could as easily have been reversed to offset displays of beautiful glassware or other kitchen collectibles.

CHAPTER FOUR

DETAILING WITH METAL

*This house is filled with metal detailing,
including a punched metal door by Isaac Maxwell
which creates an intriguing entrance.
Because of its ability to be shaped to form,
metal is remarkably versatile.*

Despite its hard and seemingly rigid nature, under the right circumstances metal is one of the most malleable building materials available. Metal's potential for diversity of form makes it one of the most challenging and satisfying materials to work with. High temperatures and forges are needed to manipulate the metal into the desired shapes and thicknesses. With a knowledge of the possibilities and personalities of metal, however, practically anything is possible.

Highly popular as an ornamental architectural feature in centuries gone by—particularly in the Renaissance, when it was commonly used as the material for highly elaborate and naturalistic altarpieces—metalwork re-emerged in the nineteenth century, when artisans were inspired by the concepts of the Arts and Crafts movement to explore various design media. With today's revival of and renewed appreciation for crafts, metalwork has once again been revived as a bold and challenging craft force.

In order to shape metal, the metalsmith will generally heat the material—iron or steel, for example—to a high temperature of 1,900 degrees Fahrenheit. This extreme heat changes the nature of the metal entirely, and it is converted from a hard substance to one that is flexible. The tempered metal can then be hammered into long, delicate forms or sculptural shapes that exude a fluidity few other craft media can match.

Because of the inherent visual heaviness of such metals as forged steel and iron, artisans in this medium frequently take unusual approaches to design. Instead of shaping the material to create a form, they might use the metal to create a frame for a shape, which consists of empty or negative space. In the process of fabricating these design boundaries, the metalsmith forges, or hammers, twists and turns into the material. This process not only creates surface interest and texture, but also

The naturalism of this lovely, brightly colored garden extends to the organic forms of the entry gate, which was made by metalsmith Greg Leavitt, above. The vinelike forms are decorated with a hummingbird motif.

produces a three-dimensional effect which adds to the overall realistic effect of the selected motif.

The malleability of metal makes it possible for the artisan to forge highly realistic forms as well as abstract ones. The work of metalsmith Greg Leavitt, which is depicted on these two pages, spans both areas. Leavitt has created a metal motif that is a perfect way to guide visitors through a beautiful garden splashed with riotous colors. Looking beyond traditional boundaries of metal design, he created a metal gate suitable for a fantasy storybook garden. Leavitt adapted the metal to create organic forms of intertwining vines embellished with a realistic-looking hummingbird drinking nectar, above. The lines of the gate are graceful and seem to yield to the wind. The fluid twists of the metal gate may cause a slight shock of recognition in the first-time visitor, upon seeing that metal can indeed be so pliant and convey such realistic imagery.

Another noteworthy example of metalwork exists inside the garden depicted. The sandbox is an informal area that is given a sense of elegance with a wrought-metal fence and gate, above right. The gate forms a delightful yet effective barrier between the sandbox and play areas. On a practical note, the gate separates the sandbox from the formal garden, which is bisected by a rambling path.

In the third example, below right, this metal gate set in a wall of masonry establishes the proper mood for entering a garden that—though carefully planned and executed—evokes the feeling of random naturalism associated with wilderness. The idea of bringing metalwork into the garden is not a new one. In the nineteenth century, metal jardinieres, plant containers, lanterns, seating, and gates proliferated in gardens. Building on these established garden traditions, all of the metalwork in this garden looks like an enchanted plant that simply sprang into existence to serve a special purpose.

That staple of childhood, the sandbox, is given a sense of unexpected elegance by the barrier formed by a metal fence and gate, above. The blend of naturalistic and abstract forms serves as a beautiful and effective divider between the sandbox, play area, and the more formal garden area, bisected by a rambling path.

Set in a wall of masonry, this metal gate creates a sense of entry to a garden that resembles a wilderness area, right.

A garden filled with water and tiger lilies is matched by a "lily" gate, left. Designed and made by metalsmith Dimitri Gerakaris, the gate measures 48 inches high and 4 inches deep and is made of forged steel and bronze.

To avoid a heavy-handed appearance, the design of the gate is formed by negative space outlined by the metalwork. This light amount of metal is, in the craftsman's words, "the salt and pepper of the structure." The individual pieces of metal have sculptural, compound curves that are forged into flowing, naturalistic lines, making the gate three-dimensional.

Just like a real lily, the metal ones on this gate have "stamens" and "pistils" at the bottom, below. These include forged bronze tips, an unusual touch, since most bronzework is cast instead.

When Christopher Ray "wove" this spider web out of forged steel, right, he created another striking gate. It guarantees privacy for the owners, who live in the Society Hill section of Philadelphia, which tourists frequent.

Made of forged iron, the irregularly shaped gate measures 7 feet high and 2½ feet wide. The idea of a spider web for the gate sprung naturally from the historic character of the area. "It echoes something that's old and musty," says the craftsman.

The threads of the web are long pieces of forged iron that wrap around one another. The surrounding frame is 1¼ inch thick and, although light, is strong enough to provide the necessary structural support. Adding to the structural support are the long vertical sides of the gate. The spider itself is a highly stylized design composed of *repousée* iron—a hollow metal form braised with nickel silver and then textured by hammering.

This lily gate, left and above, is made of forged steel embellished with bronze-tipped "stamens" and "pistils." Right, a "spider web" woven out of forged iron is the focal point of a backyard.

Symbolic of the ancient element of fire, a forged iron "firebird" decorates a security gate at a condominium development in Philadelphia. The body of the bird, above right, culminates in the head near the handle.

In both large cities or rural areas, security is an important consideration. It is of prime concern, however, in the developments in highly urban areas such as this contemporary condominium development in Philadelphia Pennsylvania. To protect the central courtyard from unauthorized entry by nonresidents, the management surrounded the residential development with a brick wall. Openings to the premises are an interesting blend of ¼-inch-thick smoked, tempered glass and an ornamental gate by Christopher Ray, above far left.

Consisting of a center gate and two side panels, the entire project measures approximately 7½ feet high and 7 feet wide. The forged iron pieces are welded together, and the gate is bolted to an anodized aluminum frame.

One of four such gates designed and made by Ray, this one is called the "Firebird" gate because of its decorative motifs. It aggressively represents the concept of fire. The other gates are evocative of the other three medieval elements: earth, air, and water. Most of the metalwork involves decorative scrolls that undulate across the face of the gate and reflect in the dark glass behind it. The scrolls form the body of the firebird motif, but instead of depicting realistic wings, they are rendered almost like flames. "It's a dual metaphor to represent the idea of fire as a source of primary energy." says Ray. The scrolls culminate at the head of the firebird, which is an extension of the gate handle, opposite above right.

To those craftspeople familiar with Ray's work, his choice of a firebird as well as the other earthly elements will come as no surprise. "It follows my background, which is based in ethnic art," he says. "I use a lot of symbols that are universal. Though they constantly reoccur in my work, they are my own variations. But the tie-in is that they are almost primal images that have been used by so many cultures over the course of history. It's like genetic memory."

While Ray's firebird gate is bursting with powerful, primal imagery, a garden gate by Greg Leavitt strikes an entirely different note, above right. Marking the entrance to a Philadelphia garden, this detail serves as a hint of the visual delights ahead. Unmistakably naturalistic in its rendering, Leavitt's gate demonstrates, in a very literal way, the fruits of the garden. This gate is designed and fabricated to include a number of motifs including vines, leaves, and tiny fruits. The organic form reinforces the environmental setting and illustrates the delicacy to which the hard materials readily lend themselves.

The sophistication of the decorative motifs and execution of the gate is belied by its rustic framing, which is vinelike in form. It blends beautifully with the rough-hewn stone wall to the rear and the naturalistic, unmanicured appearance of this deftly landscaped space.

The bounty of nature is not limited to the trees in this lovely Philadelphia garden, above. Reinforcing the naturalism is this lovely detail, a vinelike garden gate by Greg Leavitt embellished with metal leaves and fruits.

The Rittenhouse Square area of Philadelphia, Pennsylvania, is replete with houses built in the Federal style in the early 1800s. Unfortunately for the owners of this one, above, previous residents "remodeled" the façade by covering it with mundane brick in the 1950s. The owners faced a second problem as well: often when they arrived home, they discovered people hiding in the doorway. To improve both security and aesthetics by recalling the splendor that once was, the owners asked Joel Schwartz to devise a security gate and window grille that blend with the new façade as well as the other period houses on the street.

Schwartz, the owner of Schwartz's Forge and Metalworks in Deansboro, New York, responded with this eye-engaging design. Though the overall appearance of the security gate is contemporary, it ties the townhouse visually with its neighbors, all of which boast impressive period ornamental metalwork. The metal also has historic precedent in its method of fabrication. The iron is forged, not welded as is so often the case today. The process, in fact, is the same as that used for the existing ironwork in the neighborhood.

Like other examples of metalwork in this chapter, this has a fascinating interplay of negative and positive spaces. Indeed, the metal defines the negative space and, thus, the overall design.

The basis of the design is repetitive patterns that interlock. The pattern is what Schwartz characterizes as an elongated hexagon. The patterning results from taking a series of straight bars and forging them so that they

A remodeled period Federal townhouse is redeemed by the addition of a forged iron security gate and window grille, left. The material and fabrication process ties the structure to other period houses in the neighborhood. In addition, the intricate forging creates patterning as eye-intriguing as that of an Oriental rug, below left.

appear to interlock, when, in fact, they overlap. Beginning at the top of both the doorway and the window, each bar forms half of the hexagon. Then they run parallel and again move apart. The forging technique makes the bars look as if they are connected.

The effect is best seen in the detail photograph, below left. At the upper portion of the photograph, the bars are forged so that they overlap. The bars then spread apart, forming the upper portion of the geometric figure. As the bars straighten out to form the side of the hexagon, each one meets its opposite counterpart where they are forged together. Exquisite detailing is readily seen in the open area in that intersection and in the narrow banding, all of which is achieved by hand forging.

The eight bars that were used as the raw material for this intricate gate were heated to about 1,900 degrees Fahrenheit and then hammered into the desired shape. "At that heat," says Schwartz, "the metal behaves like clay, or more like plastic, than like metal."

To make arriving home convenient, as well as safe for the owners, the gate incorporates a spring-loaded lock that opens when a secret button is pushed. This way, they are freed from fumbling around with a key to get indoors.

It will come as no surprise that security is also a factor in New York City. Especially vulnerable are first-floor apartments such as this elegant pied-à-terre on Central Park West. The unusual shape of the window, an eye-riveting detail in itself, is emphasized by the grille made by craftsman Leonard Gruen, right. The metal has been molded into a variety of shapes that arc outward, creating a convex effect that brings a three-dimensional aura to the window, heightening its visual appeal. By employing an abstract form, Gruen's design does not compete with the historically derived forms used in the architecture. In fact, the metalwork actually serves as a bridge between old and new.

Historical architectural motifs on a New York City apartment building get a bit of contemporary zing by the addition of an abstract window grille by Leonard Gruen.

Structures need not be grand to be embellished with exciting metal detailing, as this simple building amply demonstrates, above. Indeed, this is a case study in the "less-is-more" theory as applied to crafts. This small addition to an existing house consists primarily of wood and is painted a contrasting color.

Large panes of glass and a deep overhang combine to create a rustic character, a look usually associated with camp-style or Swiss chalet architecture.

The basic elements have been enlivened with a metal grille by craftsman Greg Leavitt. Using naturalistic forms, Leavitt created the gate so that the design is formed by the metal itself, rather than letting open, or negative, space be defined the design.

Here the metal has been fashioned into frames for the

Swirling, leafy vines form a decorative grille on the exterior wall of a small residential addition, above. The metalwork by Greg Leavitt protects the glass windows as well as an overhead lunette. Leavitt's work can be deceptively simple as well as intricate.

two windows. Inside the frames are flowing metal roots that rise and divide into vines, which are embellished with highly detailed metal leaves. Though physically separated, the two grilles are connected visually by a series of curving metal loops that span across the face of a lunette atop the door and windows.

Another grille by Greg Leavitt proves that in the hands of a skilled craftsperson, a plain window or door opening

Hugely scaled leaves, vines, and a twisting crane convey the design spirit of this window grille, right and below. Made by craftsman Greg Leavitt, the grille spans, and gives unmistakable prominence to, two paired windows on an old brick building. A welcome change from the usual fare in security bars, this covering is both practical in keeping intruders at bay and aesthetic in bringing a sense of art to the streetscape as this abstract curving example attests, below. This grille is marked by curving spines that become right curls at the ends. Raised bandings are small touches that enhance this piece of metalwork. The spreading arc of the curved lines creates points at which the grille can be attached directly to the window framing.

can become an outdoor focal point. This undistinguished pair of windows set into an old brick building takes on importance because of these evocative iron grilles, left and above.

Unabashedly naturalistic in their design, the grilles encompass hugely overscaled leaves, vines, and other types of flora. At the top of the right window is a crane with a long, undulating neck and, at the very top, a curved head punctuated by a beak. The cranelike form is highly detailed with metal banding that gives lateral relief to this vertical design.

Equally exquisite are the large vines, intertwined with one another as well as with other, much smaller ones. The blending of large and small forms adds to the sense of realism in this artificial urban glade. In addition, the interweaving of the metalwork and the choice of large-scale elements help the grille fulfill its primary purpose of keeping burglars out.

But this grille is not only a refreshing change from the standard security bars normally used for these situations; it is also instrumental in bringing a sense of art to the streetscape and therefore, to the public.

Reminiscent of a Spanish- or American
Indian-inspired frieze is this row of
punched metal, bottom. Crafted by San
Antonio architect Isaac Maxwell, the
fixtures are made of tin-plated copper and
brass decorated with zig-zag
designs, below.

One of the more interesting, although all too often ignored, types of metalwork is the craft of punched metal. Specialized tools are used to perforate the metal with a series of small holes to make an array of patterning.

The effects that can be created with punching metal are most vividly seen in the field of lighting design. Some of the most exciting work in this area is being conducted by Isaac Maxwell and William B. McDonald of Copperworks, who run their own separate businesses in San Antonio, Texas. Both are architects, both make exciting lighting fixtures , and both also fabricate custom punched-metal doors.

Many of their motifs are regional in nature and reflect the exuberant approach to design that pervades the Southwest. Their work also evokes the spirit of the region's Spanish heritage by recalling geometrically inspired decorative motifs and punched leatherwork associated with that culture, as well as the culture of the American Indian tribes.

Inability to acquire punched-metal lighting fixtures from a Mexican supplier prompted Maxwell to begin making his own. As he explains it, "After I got out of architecture school, I started working here in San Antonio as an apprentice. I did some perforated light fixtures in one of the first houses I did. I met some people from Mexico and I wanted them to make some. But I never could get them to do that, so I started making my own." Today, Maxwell operates his own metalcraft shop that fabricates the punched designs he creates for houses built as part of his professional architectural practice.

The following several pages present a portfolio of punched-metal lighting designs, which include intriguing examples by Maxwell. In the two-story entry of a San Antonio house designed by the architect, a row of punched-metal sconces, reminiscent of a frieze, provides ambient illumination while creating an exciting light show for arriving guests, opposite below. The fixture consists of a series of sconces that measure 4 inches in diameter by 9 inches high. They are attached to a base that becomes a track concealing electrical wiring connected to a rheostat. Each cylinder is fitted with two 20-watt lamps that project light, both up and down, through the open ends.

Light also filters out through the cylinders through the punchwork on the sides. For materials, Maxwell selected tin-plated copper for the cylinders and the upper and lower portions of the base. Brass is used as banding in the center of the track. The intricacy of the punchwork craftsmanship is considerable. In the center of each cylinder is a narrow section of horizontal banding consisting of vertical rows of punched holes alternating with solid portions of copper. Above and below this row are pairs

A single sconce by Maxwell adds an exciting dash of accent lighting in a library area, above. The patterning of this sconce consists of horizontal bands decorated with motifs representative of Southwestern art that have been punched into the metal.

of zig-zag patterns reminiscent of stitches made by a sewing machine. Set parallel to each other, these patterns run around the face of the cylinder. They are flanked by additional punchwork designed in a crosshatch design.

Highly complex variations of this theme are repeated on a single sconce in the same house, above. Divided into a series of horizontal rows, the fixture is decorated with a potpourri of patterns including zig-zags and crosshatches in a variety of widths. Unlike the previous example, this sconce is effectively used as low-wattage accent lighting in a library-study area.

In fabricating the fixtures, Maxwell and his staff usually specify flat copper sheets. Patterns are drawn on tracing paper, which is then glued to the metal. After the metal is nailed to a chipboard base, the holes are punched, thus creating the patterning. The metal is then removed from the chipboard and the ends soldered together. Because the tin is subject to oxidation, the shiny surface mellows after installation to a pewter color.

Light spills out in every direction from two punched-metal sconces by Isaac Maxwell of San Antonio left and opposite above. The precise angles of one sconce radiate light out in geometric patterns, opposite right, while the curve of the other creates a halo effect. In both examples, punchwork on the face of the sconce creates a soft lighting effect that makes the fixtures glow.

A single detail can make a significant difference in the interior architecture of a room. For example, the sconces illustrated on these two pages not only serve the functional purpose of providing accent lighting, but they also attract the eye and prompt the casual visitor to pause and reflect for a while.

The sconces pictured on this page, both of which are by Isaac Maxwell, aim light directly onto the wall in a halo pattern that creates a framing effect. The punched metalwork on the faces of the sconces draws attention to the fixtures by making them glow. The geometric shape of the diamond-inspired fixture is obviously architectural in style, opposite above.

In contrast, the one above uses a softer, rounded form. The streams of light shooting out of the round portion are balanced by the downlight from the bottom, which forms an illustrated "base." The visually balanced decorative motifs of the punchwork recall the geometry of Art Deco architecture and design, here heavily influenced by the Hispanic and native American palette. (To see an example of a punched-metal door by the same craftsman, turn to page 102.)

The light covers of architect William B. McDonald, also of San Antonio, blend the visual sharpness of geometric forms with soft copper metal. Part of a line that McDonald manufactures and sells to the public via a mail-order program, these two examples illustrate two very different approaches to design.

Evocative of traditional Southwestern art, the sconce pictured opposite left is an artful arrangement of elongated parallelograms framed by zig-zag patterns above and below. To create subtle, yet visually effective, boundaries, the holes at the top and bottom of the central design are slightly larger than the others. This small difference creates small, but discernible, differences in the patterning of the light radiating outward. This sconce is a rectangle measuring 10 inches wide by 16½ inches high by 6 inches deep. It also comes in a semicircular shape with two sets of dimensions. The larger variety is 10 inches wide by 17½ inches high. The smaller one is 5 inches wide by 13 inches high. Both are 6 inches deep.

Far more contemporary in appearance is a sconce that McDonald calls the "lattice" pattern, far right. The dark areas are solid copper; the brightly illuminated strips are areas of punched metal; the top and bottom of the light cover are framed with solid bands of metal. The lattice design is available in two rectangular sizes: 11 inches wide by 16½ inches high by 5½ inches deep or 9 inches wide by 11 inches high by 5½ inches deep. In the semicircular configuration, the fixture is also sold in two sizes: 10 inches wide by 17½ inches high by 6 inches in diameter and 9 inches wide by 11 inches high by 5½ inches in diameter.

Both of these sconces project light up and down, as well as through the punched holes. Depending on the size of the individual fixture, the sconces are fitted with a single or double porcelain socket for interior installation. If the fixtures are destined for outdoor use, they are fitted with an optional clear polycarbonate rain cover.

Like most covered fixtures, punched-metal sconces are most effective when lamps or bulbs are clear, instead of soft-white or otherwise light-diffusing ones.

The work of architect William B. McDonald of San Antonio is equally geometric. The parallelogram, a staple of Southwestern design, has been elongated and framed by zig-zag patterning formed by holes punched in the thin copper skin of the light cover, left. The contrast of solid and punched metal results in a lattice design in the example pictured below right.

Attached to an old barn in Connecticut are two contemporary details: wind frames that catch the passing breeze and reflect the images of the immediate environment. On the south-facing wall, right, is a long rectangular frame that can be removed and transported to different sites. The east wall is detailed with a striking, permanently installed triangular wind frame, below. Both consist of thousands of small aluminum plates that are hinged at the top to a wire mesh grid. Their light weight enables them to waft in the breeze creating a constantly changing mural of the sky, clouds, and earth.

To succeed as art, detailing need not be deadly serious. Indeed, the best details fuse their artistry with a great deal of whimsy. In the metalwork of the imaginative craftsman Tim Prentice, art and whimsy come together on an extremely large scale.

For his canvas, Prentice chose the sides of an old barn on his property in West Cornwall, Connecticut. On one wall, he erected a rectangular environmental mural that he calls a "wind frame," measuring 42 feet long by 4 feet high, opposite above. The other wind frame is designed as a triangle, opposite below. It is 32 feet across and approximately 9 feet high.

Both wind frames are built on the same principle. Each is attached to a different wall of the barn by a grid structure consisting of wire mesh with small hooks on which are hung numerous small metal plates. When the breeze blows, the plates waver in the wind and their surfaces reflect the light.

The visual effect varies with the season, time of day, and intensity of the wind. The triangular frame, which is set on the east-facing wall, reflects the gentle morning light. The rectangular frame is sited to face south and receives intense direct sun throughout the day. In the winter, the reflection consists of snow; in the fall, the colors of the autumn foliage. All year long, however, the wind frames catch the image of the earth, sky, and clouds that appear to move across the face of the old barn. "It's sort of like vertical water," says the artist.

Prentice's inspiration for the wind frame came, in part, from a car wash. Anyone who has driven down the West Side Highway in Manhattan has probably seen this car wash, whose glittering gold metal mural emblazoned with the company name and service cannot easily be ignored by passersby.

Prentice took this lowbrow idea as a starting point to create art. In this case, the design reflects the environment, rather than a commercial message, and is dictated by the wind. The impression the wind frames make on passersby is unmistakably strong. "We're like a tourist trap up here," is the way Prentice describes it. "Lots of people see it as they drive by. Then suddenly they stop and back up to take a second look."

Though each wind frame looks monolithic when seen from afar, each is made up of many small panes of metal. In fact, the triangular wind frame consists of 2,200 plates measuring 2 inches wide and 4 inches high. Attached to the wire mesh frame by hooks at the top, the plates are extremely vulnerable to the vagaries of the breeze.

For the faces of his wind frames, Prentice selects very thin light-weight aluminum, normally reserved for industrial applications. This "mill-finished aluminum," as it is called, is not shiny, but, instead, has a finish that looks much like pewter. "It's what you get when you don't specify anything else," is Prentice's simple, but direct explanation.

Because of the dullness of the finish, the images reflected by the wind frames are not sharply focused, but are soft and diffused, even dreamlike. From large sheets of this material, Prentice and his workers cut out the desired plates and attach them to the frame.

While the effect can only be captured by the camera in freeze-frame fashion, the view by the human eye is quite different. "I have some videotapes of them and they look as if they're just boiling with constantly moving colors," says Prentice.

In addition, the rectangular wind frame is portable and can be removed from the barn wall and transported to different events, ranging from exhibitions of Prentice's work at various art galleries to rock concerts. Indeed, Prentice has taken a portable, circular wind frame to outdoor rock gatherings where it has been a decided visual hit. "People come up and say, 'Wow! It's responding to the [rhythm of the] music,' " says Prentice. "Except, of course, it's actually responding to the breeze." The portable models have the added advantage of allowing the breeze to waft between the plates, as well as across their faces, for a completely different visual effect.

While the wind frames may not be suitable for the side elevations of most houses, they make for striking conversation pieces when placed in a courtyard where their constantly changing images bridge the gap between art that is static and art that is moving.

Prentice's next installation will be slightly different. To see the effects a wind frame creates when it reflects water, he has been commissioned to erect one in the form of a tower rising out of a pond.

One of the remarkable advantages of detailing with metal is its versatility. Besides the materials you have already seen in this chapter, metal readily lends itself to a number of other applications including artful fireplace screens, interior railings, and even doors.

Consider, for example, the fireplace screen made by metal craftsman Ira Dekoven. Set in front of an arched firebox, the screen consists of fine mesh wiring that holds the fire inside and protects the furnishings in the room. Placed in front of the mesh is a decorative treatment of a realistically rendered pear tree.

Stretching from the bottom of the frame to the top of the arch, the tree is complete with a trunk, branches, leaves, and it even droops with fruit. Small support feet and handles are deftly incorporated into the design.

In a new house, metal craftsman Steven Rosenberg of Hammersmith in Stamford, Connecticut, designed and made an unusual interior railing for a second-floor stair landing, below right. Stretching approximately 7 feet wide, the metalwork is 28 inches high. For his material, Rosenberg selected steel, which he hand forged at what is called "orange heat," a temperature of between 1,800 and 2,000 degrees Fahrenheit.

The design is an undulating pattern that arcs out into space and then back. Instead of a static evenness, Rosenberg designed the railing so that the arcs change in size as they move across the face of the railing. "I've described it as a bubble existing within the screen," says Rosenberg. "The element of intrigue is born of the fact that it breaks with convention, that it does change from one end to the other."

The undulation is created by hand forging the bars with arcs of varying sizes. At each end, the arcs are only small indentations in the individual bars. Near the center, however, the arcs grow gradually in size. In addition, the ¾-inch-thick bars have been drawn out and flattened in the forged areas to approximately ⅜ inch.

The grille is set inside a frame of red oak. To the rear, a stock metal spiral staircase leads up to a cupola at the peak of the house.

Isaac Maxwell's punched metalwork, showcased in the lighting section of this chapter, is used here as a decorative door treatment for a kitchen pantry. The familiar horizontal zig-zag pattern of the Southwest has been set on its end so that it rises from the bottom of the door to the top. The pantry doors are arranged as a pair that swing out to the sides when opened from the center.

A fireplace screen by Ira Dekoven takes on decorative life by incorporating a pear tree motif, above.

A stair landing grille by Stephen Rosenberg is enlivened with an undulating pattern that begins small and grows in size across the face created by the metal bars, above.

Punched metalwork in soft colors by Isaac Maxwell is a sophisticated treatment for what is essentially a pantry door, left. Here, the pattern usually seen in lateral fashion has been set on its end to rise vertically, emphasizing the detail. The doors open in the center for access to the storage space.

The Technique of

METAL WORK

When craftsperson Steve Rosenberg of Hammersmith Iron Works fabricates a custom metal detail, he begins by carefully creating the design—in this case, a fence— in his studio in Stamford, Connecticut, left. After Rosenberg perfects the design at the drawing board, it is redrawn life-size in chalk on the floor of his studio, right. As each piece is made, Rosenberg and an assistant set the individual pieces in place over the chalk pattern to see the design take shape. The unassembled fence is removed to a work area where each detail is again laid in place, below.

The fence is painstakingly welded together one joint at a time as the design becomes a living detail, left.

Once the welding process is completed, each weld is sanded so that the final finish is aesthetically appealing and structurally intact, right.

CHAPTER FIVE

DETAILING WITH FIBER

Fiber detailing can bring an air of grace and elegance to any room. This bedroom features window treatments which Joy Wulke made with soft, translucent fabrics that gently filter light to the indoors.

Fiber details are what supply those all-important finishing touches in designing an interior. In fact, they bridge the gap between built-in architectural details, such as those illustrated in other chapters, and outright decorating.

The beauty fiber brings to an interior is important. Because it is soft, fiber offsets the stark lines of modern architecture. It imbues an all-white interior with an exciting dash of color. Fiber contrasts with smooth, sleek surfaces such as marble. And it reinforces the texture of brick and other earthy ceramic.

Compared to other materials used as details, fiber is delicate and has a shorter lifespan. Most textiles currently in use have an average practical lifespan of about fifty years.

When the owner of this remodeled house returns after a day at work, he is welcomed by a rag-weave rug by fiber craftswoman Missy Stevens that is decorated with the motif of a house.

Color is the basis on which Joy Wulke selects her materials, which can range from cotton and cotton blends to linen and even silk. Indeed, she gives silk and men's suiting material new life—not for the purposes they were intended, but instead as bed coverings and other details. Wulke's fiber work results in beautiful—and practical—window treatments that play a part in passive-solar space-heating systems and other energy-conserving contemporary design schemes.

In contrast, the rustic tradition often associated with folk art is flourishing in the craft of Missy Stevens. For a client who remodeled his old house along contemporary lines, Stevens designed and made a 3-foot by 5-foot area rug that deftly blends with the rich tones of the wood floor while contrasting nicely with the modern sloped ceiling and white walls and ceiling, above. Fabricated with a rag-weave technique, the rug has a multicolored ground decorated with the decorative motif of a warm and welcoming rendition of home. However, instead of being applied or otherwise added to the ground, the house design is incorporated into the weave so that the rug is all one piece.

The palette of the rug in Stevens's own house is far more subtle, opposite. Here, the soft, closely aligned colors echo the country atmosphere in the dining area of an old farmhouse, which she and her husband, craftsman Tommy Simpson, carefully remodeled.

Today, the emphasis in fiber detailing goes far beyond mere color to encompass the combination of unexpected and disparate materials. Textiles lend themselves to intriguing combinations and treatments. The coarseness of canvas makes it an excellent decorative foil for sophisticated furnishings. Cotton and linen, on the other hand, can be woven into a range of weights and made either smooth or coarse, enabling them to be used for floorcoverings as well as upholstery. Even silk, which we often think of strictly in terms of fashion or delicate upholstery, can be blended with other textiles into unexpected, though visually striking, bed covers and numerous other items.

Contemporary craftsmen and women are creating exciting work in fiber. As is shown in this chapter, Bee Morrow and Randy Jones transform an everyday material—commercial-grade canvas duck—into an artful canvas with colorful, hand-painted motifs to create eye-catching floor cloths. Bruce Duderstadt makes softly evocative drapery using drawnwork. In this process, Duderstadt removes, or draws out, certain threads, leaving the remaining material soft and translucent.

The area rug in Missy Stevens's dining area visually softens the rustic nature of the expanse of exposed wood while adding a subtle touch of color and design in the form of a checkerboard pattern underfoot.

Though the use of fiber is indeed a contemporary passion, fragments of old textiles, many of them from the nineteenth century, can be seen in museums, showing the impressive history of the use of textiles in the home. The collections of institutions such as the Museum of American Folk Art in New York City are enriched with handcrafted quilts, for example, that reveal our ancestors' exciting and even daring palette. These outstanding examples of folk art often combine unexpected colors, such as red and black, in visually exciting geometric designs, such as stars, that are in total sympathy with contemporary detailing.

An example of the influence of traditionalism on contemporary detailing is shown in the fact that one of the newest floor treatments is also one of the oldest. It is the floorcloth—a flat, woven textile that is a simple, yet effective, decorative floor covering. Hundreds of years old, the floorcloth is a traditional but often neglected method of visually and physically softening hard floors.

Bee Morrow and Randy Jones, the principals in Decorative Arts Ltd. in Houston, Texas, created this lovely floorcloth for a sun room in an older house. It is used as an alternative to the existing ceramic tile floor. Measuring approximately 10 by 15 feet, the floorcloth is made of heavy-grade commercial canvas duck similar in weight to that used to fabricate tote bags.

For the design and colors of the floorcloth, Morrow and Jones took their cues from the upholstery and wall coverings in the room. The floral motif on the field of the floorcloth was inspired by the wallcovering. The flowers are a stylized rendition of the design from the fabric on the walls which were enlarged and translated into painted stencils. A border of pink surrounds the off-white field, giving shape to the room. In between the field and the scattered flowers are thin lines painted in shades of grayish-pinks and greens.

The artists prepared the canvas for painting by taking it to a local awning manufacturer. There, the staff hem stitched each side using equipment specifically designed for commercial-weight textiles. To prevent the colors from later bleeding into each other and to ensure straight lines, tape was stripped onto the fabric, creating channels that were then painted. The colors are all water-based latex and acrylic paints. After it was painted, the entire floorcloth was sealed with several coats of another water-based product, acrylic polyurethane, which protects the finish without causing it to develop a yellow cast.

As a surface treatment, floorcloths offer a great deal of versatility. "The real beauty of the floorcloth is that you can put any design on it that you like," says Morrow. For example, Morrow and Jones have painted a number of artful *trompe l'oeil* effects in their work, while providing sturdy footing underneath. One of those was the painting of simple canvas to create a terra-cotta-tile effect. As a result, the homeowners enjoy the visual fantasy of an Italian courtyard in a second-floor room. And they avoided the expensive structural changes that would have been required to accommodate an expanse of heavy outdoor terra-cotta tiles.

Caring for a floorcloth, says Morrow, means following a few simple rules. To protect the polyurethane seal, the cloth should be left lying on a hard surface such as wood or the ceramic tile that already existed in this sun room. While common sense dictates laying a pad underneath, this approach often makes the polyurethane seal crack, leaving the floorcloth unprotected and subject to damage. Cleaning a floorcloth that is sealed requires only occasional damp mopping. "It's actually easier to keep a floorcloth clean than a white rug," says Morrow. In addition, the polyurethane seal shields the canvas from the ravaging effects of direct sunlight. And the acrylic paints that Morrow and Jones selected are extremely resistant to fading, which helps the floorcloth retain its original colorfulness for years.

The floorcloth boasts the one other advantage of portability. If the owners want a change of decorative pace, all they have to do is roll up the cloth, leaving the original floor exposed. The floorcloth, however, should not be folded for storage. Instead, Morrow recommends rolling it up on a standard carpet tube with the painted side facing out. This will prevent the finish from cracking and preserve the floorcloth for many years of enjoyment.

Old and new unite on the floor of a sunroom in an older Houston house, above. A floorcloth, a decorative effect that dates back to Colonial America, is rendered here in the form of heavy-grade commercial canvas. The canvas is embellished with a contemporary color scheme adapted from the room's fabric wall coverings and upholstery. In the center, an off-white field is decorated with stenciled flowers. A pink border surrounds thin stripes of grayish-pink and green, left.

The rolling skies above old Cape Cod are mirrored in impressionistic fashion in a wall hanging by Sherry Schreiber, right. The tapestry softens the look of the stark lines of the contemporary architecture and monochromatic color scheme, while imbuing the dining area with a unique sense of place. In researching her design, Schreiber photographed a number of skyscapes along Cape Cod before choosing this one as the basis for her design. To add drama to the cloud formation, the clouds were woven into the background as an overlay, which gives them a three-dimensional feeling and blends impressionistic art with realism.

Detailing with fiber creates the exciting opportunity to use textiles for a wide range of interior surfaces: floors, walls, and even ceilings in the form of tenting. While fiber wall treatments usually result in mere decoration, the two examples here show that, in the hands of a sensitive artist, they can play an important role in the interior architecture as well.

The wall hanging on this page, woven by Sherry Schreiber, offsets and visually softens the hard lines and white walls of a contemporary house on Cape Cod. Measuring approximately 4 by 6 feet, the wall hanging captures a view of a cloud-filled sky that shows what the owners see when they look out one of their windows. In fact, in preparing the piece, Schreiber developed her composition from a photograph she took of the sky on a cloudy day in Cape Cod.

In weaving this detail, Schreiber used a technique called "ombre." With this approach, the colors in the piece gradually change from the grays and off-whites in the clouds to the blue of the sky. Each line of the weft, or woven portion, consists of six yarns, all of which are varying shades of the same color. While Schreiber buys some of her yarns, she hand dyes most of them to achieve the gradations of color that she wants.

To translate a three-dimensional scene into a two-dimensional format without losing a sense of realism, Schreiber wove the clouds in a different pattern until they became an overlay. "Those clouds actually pop out a bit from the background weaving," explains Schreiber. "In a sense it is like embroidery, except that you're doing it at the same time that the background is being woven."

An added sense of texture results from the use of handspun linen that has been imported from Scandinavia. "The texture created by the linen is very important," Schreiber explains. "It tones down the architecture while at the same time dramatizing it. The piece has a softer feeling than a painting. And wall hangings in general absorb sound."

While Schreiber's work is set in opposition to the architecture, Joy Wulke's wall hanging echoes its lines, shapes, and colors, opposite. The tapestry in the living room of a ski house owned by Vada and Theodore Stanley measures approximately 15 feet by 30 inches. Consisting of fabric and wood, the wall hanging is rich in imagery. At the bottom, patches of dark fabric evoke the spirit of the nearby mountains. Above that are patches of white decorated with zig-zags reminiscent of ski trails down the mountainside. A patch of red symbolizes the mountain sunset, while an area of blue evokes the brilliant mountain skies overhead. In all, the colors range from light pinks and rose to beige and a peacock blue. To ensure the compatibility of all these colors, Wulke selected tones that include a significant amount of gray.

Throughout the piece are stenciled flowers to break up the geometry of the design. They also reflect the floral motifs incorporated in other rooms of the house. The three primary areas of the tapestry—earth, snow, and sky—also represent the architecture of the house, which spans three levels.

For structural support, Wulke incorporated a series of

A vacation ski house is filled with imagery in the tapestry by fiber artist Joy Wulke, left. The long, narrow wall hanging incorporates beiges, whites, reds, and blues to represent various aspects of the mountain environment. The white, or "snow," portion of the tapestry is enlivened with fanciful ski tracks reminiscent of the rush down the mountainside toward home.

standard pine dowels into the tapestry. Besides dowels at the top and bottom, there are several others in strategic areas of the piece that are held in place by loops of fabric. They are painted with flat latex paint.

Unlike many fiber artists, Wulke is more concerned with color than materials. "I select fabrics by colors," she says. "But this piece consists mostly of cottons or cotton blends." Wulke does want the textiles to be nearly the same in composition. "For instance," she says, "I don't want to mix a stretch material with one that isn't." All the textiles incorporated into this piece were bought off the shelf at fabric shops.

The choice of draperies for window treatments can seem terribly narrow. In fact, the selections available are usually limited to the traditional drawn draperies sold in department stores or specialty shops.

There is a choice, however, as the inventive treatments on these pages demonstrate. For example, in a dining room in a San Antonio, Texas, house, fiber artist Bruce Duderstadt fabricated an expanse of draperies that become the focal point of the space, right.

Measuring approximately 12 feet by 9 feet, these drawn draperies are made of commercially available cotton monk's cloth. The cloth has been modified so that it consists of alternating bands of loose and tight weaves that range from 3 inches to 1 foot high. The loose areas were created by removing the horizontal threads in the material, an old process called "drawn work." Then, each six to eight of the remaining vertical strands were gathered and tied in a knot to develop patterning. These decorative patterns span the width of the translucent open-weave areas.

In the solid areas, the monk's cloth was left intact. Duderstadt, however, punched through them with the same type of needle used for making hooked rugs. The solid areas are further decorated with patterns in a chain stitch. At the bottom of the draperies, Duderstadt removed the horizontal threads and tied the vertical threads in knots, forming another decorative pattern.

A quite different approach to translucency is illustrated in the living room drapery of a Vermont ski house, opposite above. Designed by Joy Wulke, these draperies fit across a bank of windows that look out onto the ski mountain. In devising the window treatment, Wulke sought to preserve the light that pours into the room from the outdoors while maintaining privacy. To accomplish these goals, she devised a system that involves two sets of draperies.

The inner layer of drapery shown here consists of a series of white nylon panels that can withstand the intense sunlight much more effectively than natural textiles. The panels are embellished with various layers of material that create an undulating pattern across the face of the drapery reminiscent of the snow-covered ski mountains outdoors.

The result is that the living room is illuminated all day by highly diffused natural light. Though sheer and translucent, the draperies provide plenty of privacy. "It works like any other translucent situation," explains Wulke. "When the light is brighter on the outside, then no one on the exterior can see inside. Yet the people indoors have an expansive view of skiers coming down the mountain." Because the ski slopes are deserted at night, privacy in the evening is not a problem. If the

owners feel the need for greater nighttime privacy, however, each panel is fitted with a second shade that can be lowered completely, obstructing the view. These are commercially available accordian shades.

This approach is particularly effective in passive solar architecture, Wulke maintains. The sheerness of the nylon enables the drapes to be closed during the day, while allowing direct sun to flood and heat the interior. This eliminates the two major complaints voiced about solar houses: excessive glare indoors and the sense that many owners have of constantly being on display to the view of passersby.

In a bedroom, Wulke took an entirely different approach to designing draperies, opposite below. Here, instead of promoting the flow of light indoors, the goal was to block it out entirely. The drapery treatment consists of a "sandwich" of layers of cotton on the front and back. In between are two layers of dense synthetic batting and a layer of mylar. As a result, the drapery blocks heat loss as well as the infiltration of light.

Common monk's cloth has been manipulated to create alternating bands of open and closed weaves in drapery by Bruce Duderstadt, left. Open areas represent drawn work while the closed bands are punctuated by openings literally punched into the fabric. Nylon panels with an undulating design by Joy Wulke maintain views and privacy in a ski house, right. Extremely thick draperies by Wulke prevent light from penetrating and heat from escaping through the windows of a bedroom, below.

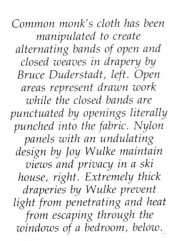

The decorative motifs on the drapery were taken from the architecture of the house. The deep salmon panels serve as a background for rectangular blocks of color, representing the various levels of the three-story house. The blocks are light salmon and various shades of blue, mauve, and beige.

The colors of the draperies are repeated on the bedspread, which was quilted by Grassroots Crafts in Lost Creek, Kentucky. The design is reminiscent of a trellis and freely blends stark geometric and curvilinear forms. Running throughout the bedcovering is a white floral pattern evocative of a rose vine pattern. The custom pillows were fabricated by graphic designer Kay Harvey of Madison, Connecticut.

Finding inventive bedcoverings presents a stiff aesthetic challenge. Because commercially available bedcoverings are often mundane in design, they represent an excellent opportunity for creative craftspeople, while adding a sense of detailing in today's houses. In the bedroom of a recently remodeled house in Connecticut, a quilt by Joy Wulke steals the show, right. It is an inviting blend of opposites. Wulke has combined the somber quality of men's tropical-weight wool suiting material with the delicacy of silk.

The bed becomes a canvas for Wulke's artistic expression. "I really saw that quilt as a painting," Wulke recalls, noting that she used symmetrical forms, including circles and squares. Though these are standard forms, they have been combined in unexpected ways in an attempt, as Wulke describes it, to "make them dance with each other." To achieve this goal, Wulke eschewed the presentation of these forms in a static, formal manner. Instead, the designer grouped them in such a way that they are slightly off-center.

As a result, the bedspread is one complete design, rather than a repetitive series of motifs as usually found on printed fabrics. At the very center is a square with lines extending outward, dividing the quilt into four quadrants. The dominant motif in the design is a circle alternating in color from gray to neutral as it circulates through each quadrant.

The materials that Wulke used in part dictated the interesting colors. The suiting material is inherently subdued in its gray tones. These are echoed by a variety of neutral hues. To create a spicy contrast, Wulke offset the predominant neutrals with a bright stripe of red in the very center of the quilt. The unexpected sprightliness of the red has the visual impact of a ribbon of neon lighting on this background.

In a different house, Wulke enlivened the contemporary spirit of a guest bedroom by using traditional forms for the bed quilt. The bedcovering itself is a standard design, hand-made by the quilters at Grassroots Crafts in Lost Creek, Kentucky. This design, called the "Sampler," is an excellent example of traditional quilting techniques preserved by Appalachian craftswomen.

In keeping with tradition, the quilt is a riotous combination of geometric and natural forms: hearts, diamonds, floral patterns, circles, and squares. This quilt, however, is startlingly different from a traditional design. It is executed in a narrow range of pale blues and beiges. To Wulke, these colors evoke the image of a changing sky and mesh well with the blue carpeting that extends throughout the interior. In addition, the monochromatic

Juxtaposition creates an interesting interplay on two very different bed quilts by fiber artist Joy Wulke. Sprightly geometric forms are rendered in somber grays and neutrals enlivened only by a stripe of neon red, above. In the other, traditional decorative motifs and a monochromatic color scheme create an air of contrast, opposite.

color scheme imbues the traditional forms with an inherently contemporary zest and creates an interesting juxtaposition of old and new.

Supplementing the quilt are two coverlets folded at the foot of the bed. Like the quilt, the coverlets are primarily pale blue interspersed with beige. They are handwoven by the very talented craftswoman Kelton Roberts of Woodstock, Vermont.

To round out the potpourri of details enlivening this bedroom is a large, insulating window quilt. It is set against the rear wall, where it covers a sliding glass door that opens onto an outdoor deck. In keeping with the rest of the room, the designs on the window quilt mirror those on the bed quilt. In this instance, however, they have been simplified so the two don't compete with each other for visual attention. Here, too, the monochromatic color scheme visually flattens the traditional designs, adding to their contemporary effect.

This window quilt is fashioned as a Roman shade that moves up and down. Because of its tight fit inside the window opening, it conserves heat and prevents early morning light from disturbing the owners' sleep.

The Technique of
FIBER WORK

Renowned for her work in
fiber, artist Joy Wulke
completes an axonometric floor
plan that will show in three
dimensions the space-planning,
arrangement of furnishings,
and details such as draperies,
above. In her studio, Wulke
examines a bolt of fabric, above
center. Some of her favorite
materials include soft,
translucent fabrics that gently
filter light to the indoors,
above right.

Working at her sewing
machine, Wulke hems the
destined material, left. The
fruits of her labor are soft,
dreamlike bed dressings.

They are embellished with cross-patching that evokes the spirit of latticework, thus combining geometric forms and inherently soft materials, above. Included in this treatment is a contemporary version of a motif that is quite historic—the graceful canopy.

CHAPTER SIX

CHAPTER SIX

DETAILING WITH
MASONRY AND CERAMICS

Custom tiles imbue this kitchen, remodeled by Dorothy Davis and located in Texas, with the air of the south of France. The combined elegance and easy maintenance of ceramic and masonry applications make these materials excellent choices for detailing on walls and floors.

Detailing derived from masonry and ceramics adds a sense of monumentality to any interior environment. Because of the size of the materials, they are usually specified for large-scale details that inherently become the focal point of a room. In this chapter, a number of contemporary details fabricated from these ancient materials are highlighted, including archways, pilasters, and brick and stone fireplaces such as the one shown here, opposite.

Crafted by Larry Neufeld, this stone fireplace is part of the interior architecture of a house designed by Neufeld's partner, architect Stephen Lasar. As a detail, the 2½-story tall and 7-foot-wide fireplace serves several important functions. First, it is a much-needed source of heat during the long winter. Second, it is undoubtedly the center of attention in the living area. Third, by separating the living area from the dining space on the opposite side, the fireplace serves as an interior space divider in the open-plan public zone. This establishes a circulation pattern into the dining area that is reinforced by the way the fireplace functions as a visual, but not structural, anchor for a stairway. Set to the side, the stairs wrap around the fireplace as they descend to the lower level of the house, where the chimney accommodates a second fireplace in the library. Finally, the lateral positioning of the stones, offset by the towering height of the chimney, directs the viewer's eye from side to side as well as upward, which has the effect of making the interior seem much larger.

Though the visual impact of the fireplace is dramatic, it is fabricated from simple materials. The structure is composed of concrete blocks, which are faced with simple fieldstone, that most common of New England building materials. Undeniably humble, fieldstone has been *the* choice for walls that mark property boundaries in the region for centuries. It has been rendered here in a highly contemporary manner that matches the architecture of the house itself.

Careful fitting of the stones ensures a naturalistic look that is enhanced by raking away the outermost cement between the stones, leaving each one exposed in relief.

Fieldstone is a material that everyone has heard of but few know the exact nature of. The reason is simple: "fieldstone" is an umbrella term covering any type of stone that is not quarried. In New England, these stones can readily be found at random in the fields, where they are a reminder of the movement of glaciers down the face of North America. In Connecticut, one of the most common types of fieldstone to be found is granite.

The material for the fireplace was harvested right on the property, which has numerous stone walls to protect the steeply sloping site from unwarranted soil erosion. By foraging on the site, Neufeld was able to select the precise stones he wanted so that they would fit together in an almost seamless fashion. "You don't know what stone you're going to use next," explains the craftsman. "You have to go out and find it. The science is seeing which is a good face and where it will fit best."

To reinforce the aura of naturalism created by his selection of the weathered stones, Neufeld fit the masonry to hide the fact that the stones are cemented together. This requires establishing a consistent amount of open space around the stones so they do not touch, or "kiss," as Neufeld describes it. The space is filled with cement, which is "raked" away at the front, leaving each stone exposed in relief, above. Though small, the opening is important in aesthetic terms as it conceals the mortar at the back and creates an interesting interplay of shadow as the fireplace is struck by light. The stones are "married" to the cement block by corrugated metal strips called "brick ties." These brick ties then stick out of the joints between the structural skeleton and into the mortar, holding the stones firmly and securely in place.

Rising to a height of approximately 18 feet, this fireplace by stonemason Larry Neufeld emphasizes the sloped ceiling of a contemporary living area, opposite.

This brick fireplace wasn't intended to double as an indoor dog house. It just turned out that way.

Designed and built by Conrad Malicoat of Provincetown, Massachusetts, the fireplace measures 8 feet wide and 7½ feet high and is approximately 3 feet thick. It wasn't even completed in this Cape Cod vacation house before it was claimed by the dog as his own weekend getaway from the rigors of city living; it was finished with him underfoot. He probably supervised every step of the construction.

The fireplace is open on two sides and serves as a space divider, separating the living area from the library beyond. As envisioned by Malicoat, an opening in the fireplace was to have served as a storage space for wood. Instead, that's the space the dog claimed.

Above the dog's den, Malicoat incorporated an old-time baking oven. When the owners wish to use it, they start a fire inside the opening, close the door, and allow the fire to die down. By the time the ashes can be cleaned out, the surrounding brick mass is hot enough for baking. After the ashes are removed, breads are placed directly in the hearth.

Since it was constructed, the fireplace has been altered. A wood-burning stove was added during the steep rise in energy prices in the mid-1970s as an attempt by the owners to conserve fuel.

This beautiful fireplace is a study in design motion, or "spontaneous eruption," as Malicoat describes it. Bricks seem to roar off on their own self-determined trajectories. Certain repetitious themes can be discerned, however, in the arches and bricks that are set on end and at various angles.

In another fireplace designed by Malicoat, this one for a bedroom, the wood storage/dog's den has been supplanted by a seat, opposite. Warmed by the heat generated by the fireplace and absorbed by the bricks, the seat makes for a convenient amenity as a place to read or simply contemplate.

This fireplace is a mammoth 8 feet wide and follows the angle of the sloped ceiling to a height of approximately 12 feet. The firebox opening is relatively small, befitting a bedroom fireplace. It is approximately 30 inches wide and arches up to a height of 36 inches.

The slope not only inspired the overall design, but also is mimicked by the brickwork, much of which mirrors, or is set in opposition to, the steep angle of the ceiling. As a result, the design of the fireplace accents the contemporary nature of the interior architecture, while injecting a welcome sense of texture and vitality and the sense of age associated with this ancient building material. In fact, the fireplace in many respects echoes the architecture of the house, which is an 130-year-old structure on Cape Cod that was gutted and remodeled inside. The exterior was left intact.

Decorative and functional, this fireplace, left, serves a number of purposes: as a supplier of heat, a space divider, a baking oven, and a dog house.

A sloping ceiling sets the tone for this triangular-topped fireplace, opposite. It includes a seat for warming up close to the fire.

With the advent of central heating, many houses lost the inherent charm associated with prominently placed and beautifully detailed fireplaces and wood-burning stoves. The energy crisis of the 1970s and the ensuing steep hikes in the cost of fossil fuels, however, prompted many homeowners to reconsider using these ancient heat sources again.

The owners of this wood-burning tile stove, right, not only have a highly efficient heating unit based on centuries of proven ability, they also own a striking contemporary artifact that delights the eye even in warm weather. It was designed and built by Ron Propst of Propst Studios in Winston-Salem, North Carolina. It stands approximately 6 feet high and measures 36 inches on its widest side, which is the one containing the firebox. The front and back actually face the walls and measure 18 inches.

Though a sturdy and large-scale piece, the stove is rendered in pale tones of off-white and cream to lighten its visual impact in the room. The adjacent walls are decorated with the same type and color of tile that is specified for the stove.

One of the most interesting aspects of this stove is that the exterior tile is not only decoration, but the structure of the unit itself. The sides are fabricated from 7-by-8-inch ceramic tiles. Each tile has a raised ridge of fired clay on the back, enabling them to be fitted together and then held in place by a mortarlike mixture of clay and sand. In addition, the tiles are wired together with spring steel connected to eight clips that are positioned on the back of each tile.

The cornice is fired in separate pieces and is assembled during construction. The base of the fireplace is laid separately, as is the firebox, which is surrounded on all but the open side with conventional firebrick.

Located in the great room of a contemporary house, the stove boasts an ancient European heritage. Here's how it works: The firebox is filled with wood that is allowed to burn for three or four hours until the surface of the stove reaches maximum temperature. Instead of wasting precious heat by sending it directly up the flue to be exhausted outdoors, the stove circulates it through a series of five chambers so that every bit of warmth is extracted. In fact, by the time air has circulated through the chambers and up the flue, so much heat has been harvested and stored that the stove is cool enough to be touched by bare hands. That translates into a 75 percent efficiency rating for this stove, compared with 55 percent for other types of wood-burning units. Indeed, the stove heats this space on one firebox of wood for a period of approximately ten hours.

An entirely different, but equally artful, approach was taken by Paula Winokur of Horsham, Pennsylvania, when she designed and built a fascinating porcelain fireplace mantel, right. Located in the living room of a remodeled house, it replaced a conventional wood mantel to become the focal point of the entire room.

Though the design appears symmetrical, it is made up of many asymmetrical elements. For example, the legs are 13 inches wide at the bottom and narrow as they rise to the shelf at the top. Several niches are rigidly geometric in form and recall, in Winokur's words, "secret places. The whole feeling of the piece," she says, "has to do with meditation and a sense of mystery."

Adding to the sense of mystery is the ragged edge of the top row of porcelains. It was created by literally tearing the clay before it was fired. An intriguing "bubbling" effect in those sections of porcelain was created by manipulating the clay by hand. After the shape was perfected, the underside was reinforced with cotton batting until the clay stiffened.

Except for small drawings, the clay was left its natural white color. The drawings look like watercolors but were made from metallic sulfates. The lack of glazing, other than for the porcelain pieces, reinforces the bone white color of the mantel and surrounds the firebox to make cleaning much easier.

Because of its whiteness, the porcelain used in this fireplace makes the piece the focal point of the room and lightens the interior. The hardness of the material makes it particularly appropriate for use in a fireplace.

A contemporary color scheme of off-whites and creamy beiges blends with a classical overtone created by the cornice on a wood-burning tile stove, opposite. Based on ancient European technology, the stove is unabashedly modern, with sleek, clean lines that are part of the stove's structure. The visual effect is enhanced by tile applied to the adjacent walls.

A mundane wooden mantel was replaced during the remodeling of a living room with this striking porcelain detail, above. The ragged edge at the top is created by literally tearing the clay before it is fired. The textural mounds in the top pieces were shaped by hand and held in place by cotton batting until the clay stiffened. Paula Winokur created this fascinating mantel.

With its unmistakable vertical thrust, this chimney stretches the two-story height of an open plan that includes a living area, dining area, and kitchen, left. It is made of fieldstones arranged to retain their naturalistic look.

With its straight upward thrust, this chimney by Jeff Gammelin of Ellsworth, Maine, is not only an effective fireplace ventilation device, it's also an integral part of the architecture. Rising two stories high, the chimney emphasizes the vertical nature of the interior of this house by drawing the eye up from the ground level to the peaked roof. A skylight extends the view even further to the clouds and sky.

Visually, the organic nature of the stone chimney works with the wood ceiling and trim to soften the contemporary lines of this new house. In addition, the chimney serves as an anchor for the corridor on the second floor, which connects the various bedrooms and provides an atriumlike view down to the first floor. On the first floor, the 4-by-3-foot fireplace becomes a circulation element in the center of a large open space containing the living area, dining area, and kitchen.

The chimney is made of local fieldstone and is primarily granite. These stones range in color from extremely light to dark pinks as well as dark lavenders and grays. These are spiced with dark basalt stones held in place by mortar. The layer of mortar is made extremely thin to create the impression that there is at least one point of contact between two adjacent stones. In truth, however, at no place does one rock touch another.

In his work, Gammelin prefers to select naturally shaped rather than quarried stones. This is particularly true for stones forming the exterior layer, or "face," of the chimney. Sometimes, stones behind this exterior layer are shaped, or "worked," as Gammelin describes it, so they will form a better fit. "Usually, we don't cut stones very much," he explains. "If we do, we try to mask that by softening the edge so that it looks like it's been weathered."

The resulting naturalistic look creates a fascinating juxtaposition of shapes within the chimney. Most stones on the face of the chimney are laid laterally and form smooth, straight sides. In the center of the face, however, they are offset by stones set at an angle. These center stones create a zig-zag line. Undulating up and down the face of the chimney, this line continually invites the eye to explore the strong vertical nature of this detail. For additional visual interest, Gammelin intersperses various sizes of stones throughout the face of the chimney, instead of limiting large ones to the lower portion as structural support.

In a skylit room, this sturdy wall by stonemason Larry Neufeld brings a bit of the outdoors inside, above right. It forms a second barrier between a sun-splashed auxiliary living area and the main envelope of the house behind the wall.

Most of the stone wall is one-story high and topped

A stone wall by craftsman Larry Neufeld adds an aura of naturalism to a bright, sun-splashed interior, above. The wall rises two stories, with the two levels connected by a contemporary spiral staircase. At night, the stonework on the first floor is illuminated by lighting fixtures recessed in the overhanging balcony. A wide doorway outlined in wood connects this secondary living area with the main portion of the interior. The wall is also punctuated by a leaded-glass window on the lower level, left. This transparent element lightens the mass of the wall and preserves the view to the outdoors.

by an interior balcony. It includes recessed lighting fixtures that illuminate the wall at night. The wall, however, rises an impressive two stories high to visually emphasize the peak of the ceiling. In the space, the two-story height of the wall is emphasized even more by a spiral staircase connecting the two levels.

Though indisputably a solid visual element in the room, its impact is toned down by several openings. These include the staircase landing on the second floor as well as a first-floor doorway and window. The doorway is lined with wood, adding to the naturalistic impression, while the window opening is filled with a leaded-glass design, above left. The window enables light to penetrate into the living areas and frames the view, yet blocks cold air from seeping inside.

The lateral layering of the stones contrasts nicely with the spiraling effect of the open-tread stairway.

Function and style combine in the work of Sandra Farrell with this innovative kitchen backsplash of tile, below. Farrell starts with standard 6-by-6-inch unglazed bisque commercial tiles. She then uses various techniques with glazing: dipping, pouring, splashing, brushing, and even squirting to form abstract decorative patterns which will then be fired in her kiln.

There is a contrasting interplay between the glazes. Each tile has between three and ten layers of glazing, which creates a vast range of textures and colors that shift as one looks at the wall. For even more contrast, some of the glazes are matte, while others are highly reflective. In some cases, Farrell applies different colors of matte and reflective glaze one over another, creating a quiet change in hue and visual texture.

"I design with tiles like a quilter designs a quilt. I work with the movement of colors across the surface to create the illusions of near and far," she says.

The extensive application of tile is also shown in two bathrooms tiled by Dorothy Davis. In the woman's bathroom, opposite above, a light look is created by 4-inch-square white tiles which have an opaque white glaze with a transparent blue glaze on top. The dark blue tile has been laid in a linear pattern that serves as "wainscoting" and a "frieze" on the walls. For the floor treatment, dark blue tile has also been used.

Blue and white were also selected as the color scheme in the man's bathroom, opposite below, but here the effect is quite different. Consisting of varying shades of dark blue and white, all the tiles are in a matte finish. Like the woman's bath, this one has the effect of wainscoting and that of a frieze. But the overall effect is less soft mainly because of the floor design, which is basically patterned on a chevron and made from dark blue tiles against a white background. As a final touch, the dark blue color treatment extends to the ceramic sink.

Strong, linear motifs and the distinctive use of colors highlight two bathrooms fitted with handmade tile by Davis Tile Techniques of Dallas. A woman's bath is outlined with embossed tiles, right. The repeated vivid blue design contrasts with a softer blue and a muted, glazed variety, displaying a range of tile possibilities and how they can be effectively matched. In a man's bathroom in the same house, below right, a chevron design rendered in dark blue tile on the floor establishes a distinctive identity. In both bath spaces, tile creates an ornamental effect reminiscent of both a frieze and wainscoting.

The backsplash in this remodeled kitchen, left, uses conventional commercial tiles arranged in an abstract design.

This classically inspired archway is unabashedly contemporary. Serving as a unique focal point for the interior of the room, it also emphasizes the doorway and echoes the geometric lines of the contemporary architecture.

The art of adding that elusive sense of "presence" to a room can take many forms. Two of the more inventive are pictured here. Both are firmly rooted in classicism, but are designed in a way that their appearance is unmistakably contemporary.

Ceramist Elizabeth MacDonald discovered a way to make a humdrum doorway a truly memorable entrance. In front of the door leading into her studio in Bridgewater, Connecticut, she placed an unusually lovely geometric ceramic archway.

The interior archway serves many design functions.

First, by framing the simple door, it gives the doorway a sense of architectural importance equal to the emphasis lavished on the entryways of historic houses. Complementing this is the demarcation the archway makes between the primary studio space seen here and the less-important storage rooms beyond. Second, inside the room the archway becomes the dominant, if unusual, focal point, fulfilling a necessary requirement for any interior space. Third, the natural ceramic material and overall gray tones contrast with the white walls of the contemporary interior design, making for an interesting interplay. And, fourth, the rectangular shape of the arch echoes the geometry of the room, created by the sleek lines of the sloped ceiling and the various exposed structural elements.

The free-standing arch soars 7 feet high and is 4 feet wide. The structural frame is made of wood concealed by a layer of small tiles. The individual tiles are 2-inch squares and are approximately ⅛ inch thick.

Though the overall color impression is gray, at close inspection one can see that the archway reverberates with a wide variety of tones. These range from peachy-pinks to greens and blues.

Adding to the overall visual effect is the highly textured nature of the tiles. Though the archway is a contemporary piece, the heavily textured surfaces give it an "aged" quality that suits its classically inspired design. "It's very antique and stonelike," says MacDonald.

The texturing is the result of an inventive technique used by the craftswoman. After flattening out the clay to the desired thickness, she textures it by rolling a tree branch over it. Then, as she holds the clay in place with a piece of wood on one side, she tears the other side. This is much like tearing a large piece of wrapping paper off a roll, although the effect created with the clay is not smooth at all.

To enhance the textured look, MacDonald presses different-colored ceramic stains into the clay while it is still damp. Next, the clay is fired in the kiln at 2,100 degrees and then soaked in a liquid acrylic that fixes the powdered pigment to the fired clay. Finally, MacDonald sprays the tile with a liquid sealant.

The tiles are placed close together on the wood frame without touching. This way, there is a tiny space around each tile that catches the shadows cast by the ceramics and adds to the textured look of the archway.

The pilaster, another classical element, was appropriated by craftswoman Constance Leslie of Providence, Rhode Island, as an architectural detail in the living room of a modern house. Fabricated from ceramic, the pilaster is located in the stairwell leading from the living room down to the first floor.

Extending 7½ feet high and 1 foot wide, the pilaster is mostly a peachy-pink color. Contrasting with this is a mottled gray-green-blue that was sponged onto the piece. Additional texturing is achieved by a particular type of kiln-firing called "raku," which is described in detail with another of Leslie's works on pages 152 and 153. The pilaster is highly glazed, creating a glossy look.

While the Corinthian genesis of the column is readily apparent in the pilaster, the capital has shells, fish, and sticks that are totally Leslie's creation. The capital has been given a matte glaze.

A stairwell is imbued with elegance by a classical column rendered as a decorative pilaster, above. The capital is a fantasy of ceramic fish and seashells.

A remodeled kitchen is imbued with the classical elegance of pilasters and a frieze rendered in ceramics, above. The design of the pilasters separating the kitchen from the dining area is inspired by the Romanesque column, while the other one is of Doric origin. The table setting echoes the fruit and geometric designs of the ceramic work.

The frieze, at right, incorporates a multitude of shapes and patterns, including a checkerboard design, balls, spheres, and cylinders that enliven the upper portion of the room. The basketweave design contrasts harmoniously with the swirling lines of the pilasters themselves.

A ceramic pilaster becomes the riveting focal point in a New York City apartment, opposite page. The capital, near right, is embellished with a variety of geometric images and a yellow-orange, restlessly twisting ribbon, which effectively unifies the design.

The shaft of the pilaster, far right, is effectively highlighted by a lavender wall, which shows off the gray tones admirably. The shaft was ingeniously created in sections by the designer, who divided a mold into several pieces so that it could be easily carried and fitted into a kiln. After the ceramic dried, it was removed from the mold pieces and laid out in sections.

For the kitchen pictured on the opposite page, architect Laura Rose of Providence, Rhode Island, took special pains to showcase the ceramic work ot Constance Leslie. Flanking the kitchen work-island are two ceramic pilasters, which are stylistically based on the Romanesque column. The capitals of the columns are playfully decorated with ceramic berries, ribbons, fans, and other effects. Overhead, a 15-foot-long, 11-inch frieze spans the width of the room. The lower portion of the frieze is decorated with individual pieces of clay set in a basket-weave pattern. A third pilaster on the adjacent wall draws attention to a window and seems to add height to the room. The design of this 8-foot-tall pilaster is derived from the classical Doric column. The color of the project—a grayish purple—results from raku firing, which causes variations in intensity in different areas.

The pilaster on this page, also created by Leslie, was made from the same mold as the Doric one on the previous page. It measures 7½ feet tall and stands in a New York City apartment. The color of the pilaster was achieved by the use of a high-gloss gray glaze and subtle pink spongework. The capital incorporates multicolored glossy and matte glazes and an assortment of interesting geometric shapes.

Leslie created the design by using the raku method, whereby clay is rapidly heated in the kiln and then placed into a "reduction environment." In this case, straw was used in this stage so that the ceramic could cool quickly. Additionally, straw often produces distinctive striated marks on the ceramic. Next, glazes were applied and the ceramic was returned to the kiln for a second firing at the same temperature. If glazes contain a significant amount of lead, as did these, the impressions made by the straw create a luster effect on the finished piece that is very striking.

These ceramic sconces, right, are decorated with intriguing geometric patterns. Made by Ceramic Designs, they are reminiscent of traditional American Indian designs.

Lighting the way home, a circular ceramic sconce becomes an intriguing exterior architectural detail, above. The geometric patterning is accentuated with colors ranging from olive green to rich terra cotta.

Visually intriguing details that can be created with ceramics need not be confined to inside the house. They should also be added as exterior touches, where they act as welcoming and enlivening features that provide a preview of the attention to detail inside the home.

The sconces shown on these pages reflect this design philosophy. All are the work of Ceramic Designs, a company in San Antonio, Texas. The visual differences between the sconces reinforce the uniqueness of each design. The sconces strikingly illustrate the inherent visual appeal created by juxtaposing two natural materials: brick and ceramics.

A grouping of white ceramic sconces contrast with tan brick, opposite page. Not only do these rectangular sconces create a subtle spot of color on the façade of the house, but also they provide a sense of textural variety.

Though monochromatic, the sconces are not static. They are decorated with geometric patterning that consists of a vertical framework at the top and bottom and an interlocking diamond motif in the center. Additionally, the geometric patterning alludes to the regional heritage of the Southwest, where geometric designs of

the American Indian have inspired a centuries-old tradition reflected in crafts ranging from textile design to pottery. The patterning extends beyond the ceramic to the brick, giving an overall effect of visual variety.

Equally at home in the outdoors is the circular sconce pictured above. Although the decorative designs on this sconce are similar to those of the rectangular variety, the visual effect of this sconce is very different because of the application of color. A rich upper band of terra-cotta coloration is combined with a deeper, natural-earth color and a rich olive green. Almost ceremonial looking, this sconce also exudes the timeless quality of traditional Southwestern design.

Like other architectural crafts, these ceramic sconces combine the practical with the aesthetic. Providing necessary exterior lighting, they also create dramatic outdoor lighting effects. The rectangular and square sconces have openings at the top and bottom, which allow lighting to pour out of each end. Additionally, tiny openings in the circular sconce diffuse light in unusual patterns.

At night, these sconces become lighted sculptures, washing the walls around them with a brilliant glow.

The Technique of
MASONRY

Larry Neufeld shapes stones by hand.

Stones are fitted in place tentatively.

Plumb measurements ensure proper alignment.

Mortar is applied atop a layer of stones.

*After setting the stone in place, Neufeld scrapes
away mortar around the front of the stones so
that they appear to lay on top of one another
without the use of an artificial adhesive.*

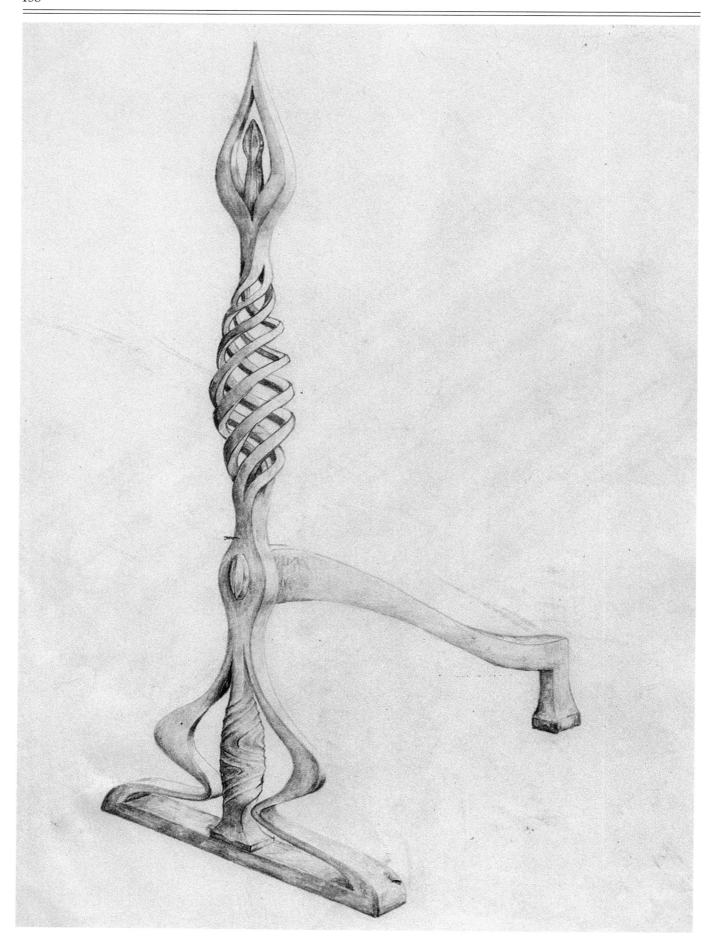

APPENDIX

WORKING WITH A CRAFTSPERSON

A competent craftsperson brings experience and skill to the detailing of an architectural element. Such a craftsperson creates more than visually striking details; he or she ensures that the work is exacting in its quality and that it meets your requirements, whether you are a professional architect, interior designer, or homeowner. And when you contract for the services of a craftsperson, you benefit from a professional's knowledge of materials, scale, shapes, and the techniques of problem solving that invariably come into play on any project.

No matter what the medium, a craftsperson should be chosen with care. You can see the range of work available at craft-oriented museums and galleries usually located in larger cities. Also, publications specializing in crafts are available nationally. A selection of these resources is included in Sources.

Because crafts are receiving more exposure than ever before, local publications can be a valuable resource. These include regional design and architecture magazines as well as the design/home furnishings sections of local newspapers. As you review publications, save articles about the sorts of items that appeal to you. Not only will this generate a list of potential craftspeople, it will give the person you ultimately choose an excellent idea of what you would like.

The process of actually contacting the craftsperson can vary considerably depending on how extensively you want the craftsperson to be involved. This can range from total involvement in design and construction to responsibility for the fabrication phase only. There are two basic approaches you can use:

—If you know exactly what you want, you can contact and interview the craftspeople of your choice and seek their bids on your project. In taking this approach, your responsibilities include three basics: you must know exactly what you want, what is practical (and what is not), and how to communicate your desires clearly. The craftsperson will need to know dimensions, materials to be used (including finishes), and deadline dates.

—If, on the other hand, you simply want an added detail that is handcrafted, you can contact a craftsperson and ask him or her to design a project and supply cost estimates. This second approach is not uncommon. Many craftspeople are very experienced in the design as well as the fabrication stage of architectural detailing. Indeed, many of the craftspeople whose work is illustrated in this book are so well known in their particular fields that they, for example, were simply asked to build a fireplace. The rest was left to their discretion. Many craftspeople are asked to take this approach even when working with experienced architects and designers, so they can bring something of their own to the work.

Business practices vary. Sometimes, a formal contract is drawn up that spells out in detail the financial responsibilities of each party. It can include delivery schedules, cost estimates, insurance, and transport obligations of the craftsperson. It also includes a fee payment schedule by the client. Many craftspeople delay any payment until after the project is completed. Others ask for an initial deposit, say, 40 percent, with the balance due on installation. Still others specify a series of partial payments that become due as phases of the project are completed: the signing of the contract, approval of the design, finishing the fabrication process, and delivery, for example.

Contracts can be informal documents, thus reflecting the more personal nature of the business relationship between the craftsperson and the client. Other craftspeople eschew contracts in favor of mutual trust. "In twelve years in this business," says glass artisan Karl Raseman, "all I've relied on has been a handshake."

Judging the quality of the work is an especially difficult job for someone not versed in a particular craft. Generally, however, wood details should be planed smooth with lines and joinery neat and clean throughout. Leaded glass looks best with neat solder lines and should be highly polished. Metal should be smooth with forged joints that are almost imperceptible to the eye. When viewing ceramic details, check for telltale cracks that can occur during firing in the kiln. Stonework looks best when the faces of the rocks are not altered by chiseling, although their look and shape may be altered on the top and sides to guarantee a better fit.

Generally, the craftsperson will interview you to get an overall idea of what you want so that he or she will have direction in terms of realistic or abstract design, motifs, colors, materials, and where the detail should be installed. Do not be concerned about seeming to be ignorant of the craft field. Many craftspeople are both comfortable and experienced in working with nonprofessionals. In fact, they often find it a refreshing change of pace from their other projects, which may be for commercial, less intimate environments.

Large details will require a floor plan indicating their placement within the room, as well as elevations, cross sections, and, sometimes, axonometric representations. The floor plan indicates the project's overall dimensions, while the cross sections show depth and height as well as the desired hardware, any interior finishes, and colors. All of these, except the cross sections, should be drawn to scale: usually ¼ or ½ inch to 1 foot. To enable the craftsperson to see precise details, cross sections as a rule are drawn to a larger scale, usually 1 or 3 inches to 1 foot. If you, as the designer, originate the project, supplying the plans is your responsibility. The craftsperson will draw separate plans for his or her designs.

If the client doesn't draw his own plans, the architect or designer will present a package to the client for final approval. It includes the drawings and plans as well as a financial budget and time schedules.

Generally, construction is considered to be the realm of the craftsperson, who has the final say over all technical aspects of the project. At this point, the client and craftsperson should be in daily contact to deal with emerging and unforeseen problems that may, for example, include uneven walls or the sudden unavailability of common materials. Out of consideration for the craftsperson, calls to the craft shop should be made before or after peak working hours.

The architect or designer's final client should also be involved during the fabrication process. Because the detail will, in most cases, be made of natural materials, clients should see them for themselves and be told of such naturally occurring discrepancies as variations in the grain of the same type of stone.

When the detail is completed, it must usually be installed and that is the craftsperson's province. The client should insist that the craftsperson be insured against damage in the transport and installation phase. It takes only a slip of the hand for a leaded-glass window, for instance, to be destroyed during movement to the construction site or during the actual installation.

SOURCES

ARCHITECTS AND CRAFTSPEOPLE

ARCHITECTS

Buchanan Associates Architects
George Buchanan
730 Main St.
Branford, Conn. 06405
(203) 488-6383

Fischer-Smith & Associates
320 Kearney Ave.
Santa Fe, N. Mex. 87501
(505) 988-3385

Kfoury Weinschenk, Inc.
Ric Weinschenk
19 South St., C-1
Portland, Maine 04101
(207) 761-4701

Robert W. Knight, Architect, Ltd.
Beech Hill Road
Blue Hill, Maine 04614
(207) 374-2845

William Lipsey
Box 3203
Aspen, Colo. 81611
(303) 925-3734

Mackall and Dickinson
26 Commerce Dr.
North Branford, Conn. 06405
(203) 488-8364

Eldred Mowery
Rt. 3, Box 175
Murphy, N.C. 20906
(704) 837-9406

Randall T. Mudge
Box A174
Hanover, N.H. 03755
(603) 795-4676

Herbert Newman
300 York St.
New Haven, Conn. 06511
(203) 772-1990

Quinn Associates
114 W. Main St.
New Britain, Conn. 06501
(203) 224-2628

Harry Teague
210 S. Galena St.
Aspen, Colo. 81611
(303) 925-2556

Christopher Woerner
299 Thimble Islands Rd.
Branford, Conn. 06504
(203) 488-7969

Zuberry Associates
Anthony Zunino
311 W. 43rd St.
New York, N.Y. 10036
(212) 307-7890

CERAMISTS

Davis Tile Techniques, Inc.
Dorothy Davis
827 Exposition Ave.
Dallas, Tex. 75226
(214) 826-5130

Brick Breakthroughs
Conrad Malicoat
312 Bradford St.
Provincetown, Mass. 02657
(617) 487-0214

Constance Leslie
369 Hope St.
Providence, R.I. 02906
(401) 351-4664

Elizabeth MacDonald
Box 205
Bridgewater, Conn. 06752
(203) 354-0594

Propst Studios
Ron Propst
209 W. Sixth St.
Winston-Salem, N.C. 27101
(919) 724-7153

Sandra Salem Farrell
Peep Toad Mill
P.O. Box 108
East Killingly, Conn. 06243
(203) 774-8967

Paula Winokur
435 Norristown Rd.
Horsham, Pa. 19044
(215) 675-7708

DECORATIVE PAINTERS

Decorative Arts Ltd.
Bee Morrow
Randy Jones
2011 S. Shepherd
Houston, Tex. 77019
(713) 520-1680

FIBER ARTISTS

Bruce Duderstadt
320 King William St.
San Antonio, Tex. 78204
(512) 223-4414

Sherry Schreiber
Box 494
Wainscott, N.Y. 11975
(516) 537-2459

Joy Wulke
85 Willow St.
New Haven, Conn. 06511
(203) 787-5867

Dorothy Davis, above left.
Elizabeth MacDonald, right.

GLASS ARTISTS

Howard Ben Tré
115 Elton St.
Providence, R.I. 02906
(401) 274-6755

Beyer Stained Glass
Joe Beyer
6915 Greene St.
Philadelphia, Pa. 19119
(215) 848-3502

Dale Chihuly
1124 Eastlake Ave. E.
Seattle, Wash. 98109
(206) 682-2684

Creative Glass Works
Karl Raseman
Vincent Winsch
59 Main St.
Setauket, Long Island, N.Y. 11733
(516) 689-7897

Cummings Studios
182 E. Main St.
North Adams, Mass. 01247
(413) 664-6578

A.J. Garber
24 Bishop St.
New Haven, Conn. 06511
(203) 777-0910

Sylvan Garrett
2501 Oak Lawn Ave.
Dallas, Tex. 75219
(214) 522-2883

Ray King
603 S. Tenth St.
Philadelphia, Pa. 19147
(215) 627-5112

Cynthia Legere
285 Mitchell Rd.
Cape Elizabeth, Maine 04107
(207) 799-2011

Mark McDonnell
12 Rhode Island Ave.
Providence, R.I. 02906
(401) 331-2958

Edward McIlvane
235 Promenade St.
Providence, R.I. 02908
(401) 274-6909

Sandy Moore
105 Wauwinet Trail
Guilford, Conn. 06437
(203) 457-1435

Maya Radoczy Designs
P.O. Box 31422
Seattle, Wash. 98103
(206) 547-7114

Janet Redfield Stained Glass
Cape Rosier Rd.
Harborside, Maine, 04642
(207) 326-4778

Kenneth von Roenn
156 Crescent Ave.
Louisville, Ky. 40206
(502) 897-5671

David Wilson Design
Rt. 2, Box 121A
South New Berlin, N.Y. 13843
(607) 334-3015

METALSMITHS

DeKoven Forge
Ira Dekoven
5820 Davis Rd.
Walkertown, N.C. 27051
(919) 744-0067

Dimitri Gerakaris
Metalsmith
Upper Gates Rd.
North Canaan, N.H. 03741
(603) 523-7366

Hammersmith
Steve Rosenberg
148 Old Ridge Rd.
Stamford, Conn. 06930
(203) 329-8798

Isaac Maxwell
129 Crofton
San Antonio, Tex. 78210
(512) 227-4752

Chris Ray, right.

WOODWORKERS

Tim Prentice
130 Lake Rd.
West Cornwall, Conn. 06796
(203) 672-6728

Christopher Ray
315 E. Wister St.
Philadelphia, Pa. 19144
(215) 438-7129

Schwartz's Forge and Metalworks
Joel Schwartz
P.O. Box 205
Deansboro, N.Y. 13328
(315) 841-4477

Upper Bank Forge
Greg Leavitt
S. Orange St.
Box 486
Media, Pa. 19063
(215) 565-3224

Dale Broholm, above.

Breakfast Woodworks
26 Commerce St.
North Branford, Conn. 06405
(203) 488-8364

Dale Broholm
63 Paul Gore St.
Jamaica Plain, Mass. 02130
(617) 522-2206

Scott Dickerson/Furniture
117 Cape Rosier Rd.
Harborside, Maine 04642
(207) 326-4778

Tage Frid
96 Daniel Dr.
North Kingsford, R.I. 02852
(401) 294-9987

Tom Luckey
210 Clark St.
Branford, Conn. 06405
(203) 481-9780

Robert Phipps
101 Harrison St.
New Haven, Conn. 06511
(203) 387-4420

Bob Trottman
Route 1, Box 100A2
Casar, N.C. 28020
(704) 538-8236

Ed Zucca
Meehan Rd.
Woodstock, Conn. 06281
(203) 974-2704

STONEMASONS

Freshwater Stone & Brick Work
Jeff Gammelin
RFD 5
Ellsworth, Maine 04605
(207) 667-4593

Brick Breakthroughs
Conrad Malicoat
312 Bradford St.
Provincetown, Mass. 02657
(617) 487-0214

Neufeld—Lasar Design Build Co.
Larry Neufeld
20 Bennett St.
New Milford, Conn. 06776
(203) 355-3765

DETAILS THAT CAN BE BOUGHT

ARCHITECTURAL SALVAGE YARDS

SUE ROSE

Northeast

Great American Salvage Yard
3 Main St.
Montpelier, Vt. 05602
(802) 223-7711

United House Wrecking Corp.
328 Selleck St.
Stamford, Conn. 06920
(203) 348-5371

Mid-Atlantic

Architectural Antiques Exchange
709–215 N. Second St.
Philadelphia, Pa. 19123
(215) 922-3669

Baltimore City Salvage Depot
213 W. Pratt St.
Baltimore, Md. 21201
(301) 396-4599

Gargoyles Ltd.
512 S. Third St.
Philadelphia, Pa. 19147
(215) 629-1700

Irreplaceable Artifacts
526 E. 80th St.
New York, N.Y. 10022
(212) 288-7397

Urban Archaeology Ltd.
135 Spring St.
New York, N.Y. 10022
(212) 431-6969

Webster's Landing
475–81 Oswego Blvd.
Syracuse, N.Y. 13202
(315) 425-0142

Central

Art Directions
6120 Delmar Blvd.
St. Louis, Mo. 63112
(314) 425-0142

Salvage One
1524 S. Peoria St.
Chicago, Ill. 60608
(312) 733-1198

Structural Antiques
3006 N. Classen Blvd.
Oklahoma City, Okla. 73106
(405) 528-7734

South

The Bank Antiques
1824 Felicity St.
New Orleans, La. 70015
(504) 523-6055

West

Architectural Emphasis Inc.
5701 Hollis St.
Emeryville, Calif. 94608
(415) 654-9520

The Architectural Salvage Co.
727 Anacapa St.
Santa Barbara, Calif. 93101
(805) 965-2446

To the trade only.

MANUFACTURED DETAILS

Aluminum Fabricators, Inc.
Highway 68
P.O. Box 267
Greensburg, Ky. 42743
(502) 932-7091

Architectural Paneling*
979 Third Ave.
New York, N.Y. 10022
(212) 371-9632

Bendix Moulding
235 Pegasus Ave.
Northvale, N.J. 07647
(201) 767-8888

Dovetail Inc.
Box 1669–131
Lowell, Mass. 01853
(617) 454-2944

Felber Inc.
P.O. Box 551
110 Ardmore Ave.
Ardmore, Pa. 19003
(215) 642-4710

Focal Point
2005 Marietta Rd., NW
Atlanta, Ga. 30318
(404) 351-0820

Gregor's Studio
3315 McKinney Ave.
Dallas, Tex. 75204
(214) 744-3385

Moultrie Manufacturing Co.
Moultrie, Ga. 31768
(800) 841-8674

Renovation Products
5302 Junius
Dallas, Tex. 75214
(214) 827-5111

CRAFTS RESOURCES

GALLERIES

John Berggruen Gallery
228 Grant Ave.
San Francisco, Calif. 94108
(415) 781-4629

Clay & Fiber
Box 22
Taos, N. Mex. 87571
(505) 758-8093

Garth Clark Gallery
170 South La Brea
Los Angeles, Calif. 90036
(213) 939-2189

Contemporary Crafts Gallery
3934 Southwest Corbett
Portland, Oreg. 97201
(503) 223-2654

Charles Cowles Gallery, Inc.
420 West Broadway
New York, N.Y. 10012
(212) 925-3500

del Mano
11981 San Vicente
Los Angeles, Calif. 90049
(213) 476-8508

Helen Drutt Gallery
1791 Walnut St.
Philadelphia, Pa. 19103
(215) 735-1625

The Elements
14 Liberty Way
Greenwich, Conn. 06830
(203) 661-0014

Elizabeth Fortner
1114 State St.
Santa Barbara, Calif. 93101
(805) 966-2613

Gallery Eight
7464 Girard Ave.
La Jolla, Calif. 92037
(619) 454-9781

Gallery 10
7045 Third Ave.
Scottsdale, Ariz. 85251
(602) 994-0405

Habatat Galleries
28235 Southfield Rd.
Lathrup Village, Mich. 48076
(313) 552-0515

1090 Kane Concourse
Bay Harbor Islands, Fla. 33154
(305) 865-5050

Hand and the Spirit
4222 N. Marshall Way
Scottsdale, Ariz. 85251
(602) 949-1262

Handcrafters
227 Galisteo
Santa Fe, N. Mex. 87501
(505) 982-4880

The Heller Gallery
71 Greene St.
New York, N.Y. 10012
(212) 966-5948

Mariposa Gallery
113 Romero St. N.W.
Albuquerque, N. Mex. 87102
(505) 842-9097

Perception Galleries
2631 Colquitt
Houston, Tex. 77098
(713) 527-0303

Signature
3267 Roswell Rd.
Atlanta, Ga. 30305
(404) 237-4426

Snyderman Gallery
317 South St.
Philadelphia, Pa.
(215) 238-9576

Ten Arrow
10 Arrow St.
Cambridge, Mass. 02138
(617) 876-1117

The Workbench
470 Park Ave. S.
New York, N.Y. 10016
(212) 481-5454

MUSEUMS

American Craft Museum
44 W. 54rd St.
New York, N.Y. 10020
(212) 397-0630

The Asia Society, Inc.
725 Park Ave.
New York, N.Y. 10021
(212) 288-6400

California Crafts Museum
900 North Point
Ghirardelli Square
San Francisco, Calif. 94019
(415) 771-1919

The Corning Glass Museum
1 Museum Way
Corning, N.Y. 14830-2253
(607) 937-5371

Craft and Folk Art Museum
5817 Wilshire Blvd.
Los Angeles, Calif. 90036
(213) 937-5544

Everson Museum of Art
401 Harrison St.
Syracuse, N.Y. 13202
(315) 474-6064

John Michael Kohler Arts Center
P.O. Box 489
Sheboygan, Wis. 53082-0489
(414) 458-6144

National Ornamental Metal Museum
374 W. California
Memphis, Tenn. 38106
(901) 774-6380

The Renwick Gallery
National Museum of American Art
Smithsonian Institution
Washington, D.C. 20560
(202) 357-1300

Textile Museum
2320 S. Street N.W.
Washington, D.C. 20008
(202) 667-0441

PUBLICATIONS

AMERICAN CRAFT
American Craft Museum
44 W. 53rd St.
New York, N.Y. 10020
(212) 397-0630

CERAMIC ARTS & CRAFTS
30595 West 8 Mile Rd.
Livonia, Mich. 48152
(313) 477-6650

CRAFT INTERNATIONAL
247 Centre St.
New York, N.Y. 10013
(212) 925-7320

FIBERARTS
Nine Press
50 College St.
Asheville, N.C. 28801
(704) 253-0468

FINE WOODWORKING
Taunton Press
63 S. Main St.
Newtown, Conn. 06470
(203) 426-8171

GLASS WORKSHOP
Box 244
Norwood, N.J. 07648
(201) 768-7055

METALSMITH
6707 N. Santa Monica Blvd.
Milwaukee, Wis. 53217
(414) 351-2232

WOODSMITH
2200 Grand Ave.
Des Moines, Iowa 50312
(515) 282-7000

WOODWORKER'S JOURNAL
25 Town View Drive
New Milford, Conn. 06776
(203) 355-2694

WORKBENCH
4251 Pennsylvania St.
Kansas City, Mo. 64111
(316) 531-5730

RESOURCE CENTERS AND ART CONSULTANTS

Creative Arts Workshop
80 Audubon St.
New Haven, Conn. 06511
(203) 562-4927

Susan Daniel
Art Consultant
607 Chapel St.
New Haven, Conn. 06510
(203) 777-8865

Southeastern Center for Contemporary Art
750 Marguerite Dr.
Winston-Salem, N.C. 27106
(919) 725-1904

Southwest Craft Center
300 Augusta St.
San Antonio, Tex. 78205
(512) 224-1848

INDEX

References to illustration captions are printed in italic type.